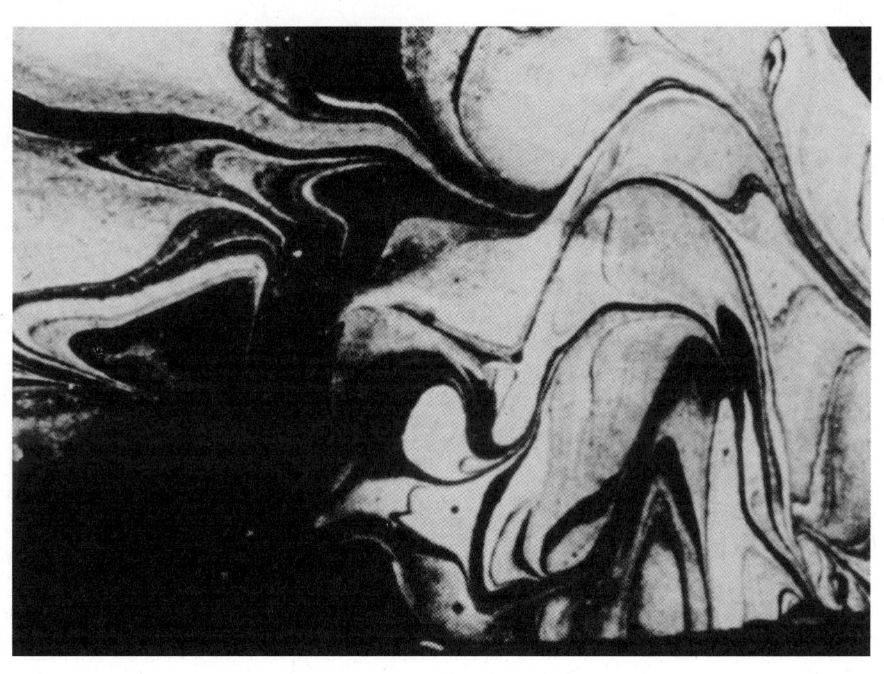

SEVEN FILMS BY PAUL SIETSEMA

MOUSSE PUBLISHING

PAUL SIETSEMA

OVERLY ARTICULATED CLOCKS
MICHAEL NED HOLTE

Michael Ned Holte is a writer, independent curator, and member of the art program faculty at the California Institute of the Arts.

I cannot remember whether or not Paul Sietsema wears a wrist-watch. To be honest, I've never thought to notice in the decade and a half I've known him. Perhaps he used to wear a watch, but no longer does. And perhaps it doesn't really matter: Most of us carry a timekeeping device in our pocket or elsewhere in close proximity to our bodies, or at least we have since mobile phones became the stuff of everyday life. The question unexpectedly crosses my mind while watching *At the hour of tea* (2013), a 16-millimeter film that features images of an ornate pocket watch, a perpetual desk calendar, a Royal typewriter, and stationery edged in black: things that immediately conjure the word "obsolescence" and the temporal expansion it implies.

Obsolescence, of course, is not the same as "obsolete"—especially not in our Google-Wikipedia-eBay epoch when nearly any artifact of industrial culture can be retrieved visually, if not purchased. Inevitably, the film itself, a spooled 16-millimeter print, projected by virtue of a flapping shutter, similarly evokes a sense of obsolescence—the slow, gradual fade-out of the mechanical age. Then, I discover an interview with Paul that contains the curious phrase "overly articulated clocks":

> If I see physical things from the two long-term projects I have made—*Empire* (2002), which was around four years of work, and *Figure 3* (2008), which was closer to five—I'm taken back to the time in which I made those things. It may have been the lack of my engagement to the time of the present outside the studio that heightened this phenomenon. The projects became a little like overly articulated clocks, meting out the time outside of time, and in some way recording things as they happened in the various steps of the daily work I undertook in the studio.[1]

The phrase in question—"overly articulated clocks"—might be as good a short description of Paul's films as any. And more generally, it hints at the operations of his larger body of work, which includes exquisitely rendered drawings and paintings of everyday objects found in his studio, or perhaps any studio. I am also struck by his phrase "time outside of time"—seemingly a philosophical conundrum, but one that goes a long way toward explaining how a temporal

1. Adam Szymczyk and Quinn Latimer, "Impossibly Clean Models: Paul Sietsema in Conversation," in *Paul Sietsema: Interviews on Films and Works*, ed. Quinn Latimer (Berlin: Sternberg Press, 2012), 94.

understanding of Paul's process of making films can never precisely align with a viewer's experience of watching one. Or at least I assume that's true.

"Few artists luxuriate in time as much as Sietsema," I recently claimed, but surely I was projecting my own experience of watching his films onto his experience of making them. I imagine his process as, almost inevitably, a kind of struggle in slow motion—the "meting out" over four years, or five.[2] Despite this slowness, the end product hardly looks like a struggle. With the word "luxuriate," I simply meant to suggest that his films demand our full attention, but also that they (or he, I suppose) make(s) no apology for demanding it. The viewer has a job to do, too, in the face of this situation. Paul's films—eight of them so far, since 1998—demand our attention and propose the possibility of slowness in a culture that by all accounts is increasingly accelerated and distracted, always looking elsewhere.

I initially encountered Paul's work in 2000, when his first film, *Untitled (Beautiful Place)* (1998), was included in an exhibition of new Los Angeles sculpture.[3] I only saw it once, and my memory of the experience of watching it is hazy, but my understanding of his work was certainly informed by the context of his time and place. The artist Charles Ray, an influential mentor to some of the most compelling artists in Los Angeles at the turn of the millennium, described the work of his students, including Paul, as "re-enchanting the world."[4] I met Paul during this period of re-enchantment. He was researching Baroque ornamentation for his next project, and I was working at a Santa Monica bookstore that sold books on art and architecture.

That eventual project was *Empire*, a 24-minute film, and I remember seeing it at least three times when it was first exhibited in Los Angeles in September 2002. *Empire* coincided with my return to graduate school, and it became the subject of my first writing in an academic context in some seven years. That text no longer exists, as far as I know, but I remember a few small details of what I wrote. First, it was in sections, perhaps as an attempt to parallel the film's episodic structure, which includes a grasshopper coming into focus; a

---

2. Michael Ned Holte, "Best of 2013," *Artforum International* (December 2013), 242–43.
3. The exhibition was *Mise-en-Scène—New L.A. Sculpture*, curated by Bruce Hainley and Carole Ann Klonarides, Santa Monica Museum of Art, June 20–August 19, 2000.
4. Dennis Cooper, "Too Cool for School," *Spin* (July 1997), 86–94, reprinted in Dennis Cooper, *Smothered in Hugs: Essays, Interviews, Feedback, and Obituaries* (Harper Perennial, 2010).

scaleless, white, cavelike form traced by a roving camera; two different crystalline structures, rotating; Clement Greenberg's apartment, circa 1964; and the Hôtel de Soubise—all (re-)constructed by the artist for the camera. Second, it was a slightly cranky account of my experience of watching the film. I remember being jarred by each splice in the film, likely the result of sitting next to the projector. Its steady mechanical unspooling was impossible to ignore, even unnerving. As I recall, there was no looping mechanism; the film was periodically rewound and started again by the gallery attendant. Its materiality was insistent.

My essay attempted to account for this insistence. Much of it was description—albeit a description of a sequence of complex images that mostly resisted the circumscription of language. (Paul's films still resist exact verbal apprehension, some even more than *Empire*). Frustrated as I was, I nevertheless stuck around to see the film several more times before endeavoring to write about it. Looking back, I suspect I was unsettled by it because it didn't conform to my understanding of what a film is, or could be. I kept expecting it to be a "structural" film, by which I mean the type of film defined by P. Adams Sitney.[5] And while *Empire* certainly has *a* structure, that structure is not its dominant characteristic. Rather, I'd say it presents a variety of complex visual phenomena that practically force viewers to *perceive themselves perceiving* the images and the remarkable differences from one viewing experience to the next. An important lesson emerged from this experience of Paul's film, coinciding with my shift from amateur art viewer to professional(izing) critic: I began to analyze things as they actually are rather than as they "should" be. I am a better viewer for it.

Inevitably, my experience of the film today is not the same as that initial encounter a dozen years ago. Each encounter is necessarily different, but also determined in large part by earlier encounters, creating a kind of aggregated perception in the imagination, a form of understanding over time. The film itself is not the work, the artist will point out: "The experience of the film, memory of the film,

---

5. Sitney defined Structural film, as exemplified by the work of Hollis Frampton, Michael Snow, Ernie Gehr, and others, as "a cinema of structure in which the shape of the whole film is predetermined and simplified, and it is that shape which is the primal impression of the film. The structural film insists on its shape, and what content it has is minimal and subsidiary to the outline." See P. Adams Sitney, *Visionary Film: The American Avant-Garde, 1943–2000* (Oxford and New York: Oxford University Press, 2001), 348. The film begs comparison to Andy Warhol's film of the same name, which seemingly meets the criteria for Sitney's notion of structural film.

embeddedness of the experience of the film in the memory in all of its spatial, aesthetic, anachronistic complexity is the work," he tells me.[6] A clock is not the same thing as time.

"At the heart of Sietsema's investigation," Chrissie Iles writes in her thorough analysis of *Empire*, "is the construction of visual perception, as experienced through a space which, as Sietsema observes, could be described in Kantian terms as 'a pure form of sensibility, which exists in the mind a priori, as the frame within which all experience occurs.'"[7] I think this remains true. Paul's films reveal an acute awareness of the frame—historically governed by industrial standards—and embrace that container as a given.[8] The frame articulates a fragment from the world around it and turns that fragment into a metonym for the world, whether or not the image in the frame is immediately legible.

I am struck by how often the images in Paul's frames only become legible over time or hover at the threshold of legibility, suspended in a process of becoming. *Figure 3*, the film that follows *Empire*, presents a series of artifacts or fragments of objects against a black ground. We can name some of them: coins, rope, netting, pottery shards. But just as many deflect or evade language, or evoke an entropic vocabulary of ruin: dust, detritus, debris, and so on. Likewise the splatters and smears in *Anticultural Positions* (2009), a film that gradually reveals these marks as the residue of the artist's production—the work outside of the work, one might say—accrued on a table in the studio. We are never shown the studio, only localized sections of this palimpsest, a kind of incidental mess revealed in clusters of close-up black-and-white shots alternating with a text written in the first person but largely borrowed from the artist Jean Dubuffet.

Whether or not we are meant to read this text—the film—as an autobiographical confession is beside the point. The worktable is understood as a historical device, and perhaps also an allegorical one—a device that inevitably embeds the artist into a matrix of labor. I'm

6. Email to the author, May 21, 2014.

7. Chrissie Iles, "Empire: A Catalogue Raisonné of an Explorer of Space" in *Paul Sietsema: Empire* (New York: Whitney Museum of American Art), 1.

8. In this sense, Sietsema's approach to film's industrial standards does parallel the concerns of Structural film as Sitney defined it. Sietsema was a student of Morgan Fisher while at UCLA, and Fisher's remarkable 16-millimeter film *Standard Gauge* (1986) offers a close analysis of film gauges used by the motion picture industry, highlighting a variety of still frames. As a curious corollary, it's also worth noting that Sietsema's recent paintings of common studio tools begin with an existing frame as a given by repurposing the backsides of found oil paintings.

reminded of the art historian Leo Steinberg's term "flatbed picture plane," a notion he located in the sand-clotted surfaces of Dubuffet's paintings and especially in the dense accumulations of Robert Rauschenberg's Combines: "It seemed at times that Rauschenberg's work surface stood for the mind itself—dump, reservoir, switching center, abundant with concrete references freely associated as in an internal monologue—the outward symbol of the mind as a running transformer of the external world, constantly ingesting incoming un-processed data to be mapped in an overcharged field."[9] For Steinberg, the flatbed picture plane was culture itself, in a state of flux.

In all of Paul's films since *Empire*, the tabletop emerges as an important framing device, an implied if not explicit ground where vision can land. (This is also true of his paintings and drawings, where the surface of the canvas or paper is understood as a stand-in for a flat, horizontal plane, even when hung vertically.) In *Encre chine* (2012), objects in the studio are slathered with a viscous coat of the black Chinese ink that gives the film its name. Many of these objects are nameable—the lid of a paint can, a hammer, a camera, picture frames, and so on—but the tarry coating begins to level difference and render the familiar strange. The accumulated objects, apparently "black" yet highly reflective from our mediated vantage point, begin to read as an undifferentiated totality in which frame and surface are one, insinuating a more expansive flood of data beyond the edges of what's made visible by the camera. I imagine a joke about watching paint dry that plays out over the 15 minutes of *Encre chine*—a dura-tion that might seem interminable to some viewers.[10]

Slowness, of course, is relative. In watching (and re-watching) these films, I've noticed how I begin to embrace their peculiar speed, or lack thereof, just at the moment they come to an end. Which is to say the end often comes as a surprise: Paul's films never offer the climax or dénouement expected of conventional narratives, yet it is also true that the ending is never arbitrary.

I began with the question about a wristwatch because I have come to understand Paul's primary project as a consideration of time

---

9. Leo Steinberg, "Other Criteria" in *Other Criteria* (London: Oxford University Press, 1972), 55–91.
10. I think of my younger students and their palpable discomfort when I screen Yvonne Rainer's *Hand Movie* (1966), with its sequence of tightly framed hand move-ments choreographed by the hospitalized dancer. One person's sense that nothing is happening is another person's sensory overload. Does Yvonne ever repeat a gesture? I'm mesmerized by that hand.

and how we apprehend it. "Perception," he once observed, "exists only in the present."[11] Likewise the perception of watching a film, with the present defined through a constant negotiation between the regular, mechanical rate of the projection—the instant of a single frame within a continuous flow—and the relative temporality of the viewer's body: Its time becomes my time, and overtakes me. And as the film endures in my memory, yet another new sense of time emerges. It's not necessary to claim that Paul's films reward our "undivided" attention, which is clearly true for this viewer. This kind of perception is obsolescent, if not already an artifact in the present. In this sense, these films embrace impossibility.

11. Gintaras Didžiapetris and Paul Sietsema, "Interview," *The Federal* (October 2011), 21–28; reprinted in *Paul Sietsema: Interviews on Films and Works*, 7–24.

THE ETCHED SIDE OF THE IMAGE
SARAH ROBAYO SHERIDAN

Sarah Robayo Sheridan is a writer and teaches curatorial practice. She is curator of exhibitions at The Power Plant, Toronto.

Film stocks come in many varieties, but they share the essential physical feature of a base plastic covered in emulsion, a thin gelatin coating in which images imprint. To handle film is to directly touch the contours of images, forms etched by the scattering of silver particles suspended in a protein made by boiling animal skin, tendons, ligaments, and bone. The image is carved into the membrane not by a hammer's blow but by the burn of light. If this sounds like alchemy, it is.

Paul Sietsema compounds organic and artificial detritus in all his artwork, scavenging in history's wake to identify specific tools of cultural production and foraging for concepts of art promulgated in the words of artists and attitudes of critics. He mines film as a vestige, the medium of the mechanical age, pressing and squeezing its very obsolescence through a contemporary sieve. In so doing, the artist hovers in the switchover between a bodily inscription in the image and a fundamental reconstitution of sight and representation in the matrix of the virtual. Where body stops and image starts is a divide collapsing through a series of innovations and accidents that go back as far as the people of Pompeii trapped in an emulsion that marked their death, but which paradoxically carried forward their image into eternity.

Sietsema's 16-millimeter silent film *Encre chine* (2012) conjures Pompeii, but in objects. Various analog imaging apparatuses encounter an oil slick that fixes another image in place, a death mask, the ancestral portrait that the Romans called *imago*. Encased in tarry ink, a hammer rests amid camera bodies, lenses, and picture frames, the whole constituting a memento mori for the hard tools of analog photography. In English this viscous fluid is India ink, in French, *encre de Chine*. Playing up this cultural discrepancy produced by differing colonial histories, Sietsema offers us the mixed nomenclature "Encre chine." Whether in his ink drawings that can be mistaken for photography, or in the uncanny verisimilitude of the constructed objects in his films, material and linguistic categories are always under siege in the artist's repertoire. In his densely layered output, we trip over the ontology of the image in a slow reveal akin to the magical release of a latent image coming into visibility in the darkroom. In the construct of the film loop, however, all catharsis is evanescent, all tropes repeat, and all ideas return, remix, and superimpose.

The writing of the material of the world onto the thin skin of film is an arduous process. Frame line, focal length, exposure time, chemistry, and the final suture of the editing process conspire in a clunky workflow that asserts the boundary between seeing the world and producing it. All of Sietsema's artworks involve the question of duplication, a process that is at the very heart of film, a medium that, like plaster casting, also engenders the production of serial forms. Sietsema engineers objects specifically to populate the shadow world of film projection.

This impulse can be traced back to his first film, *Untitled (Beautiful Place)* (1998), in which he sculpted intricate flowers from paper, paint, and clay to be photographed in various now defunct film stocks. In the lapse of this discontinued palette, we confront the instability of color taxonomy, a construct that is subject to periodic renegotiation. Flora are not simply the property of nature but clearly the designate of culture; the English garden and the ikebana arrangement are examples of nature filtered through precise and subjective aesthetic imperatives. Sietsema's drive to make likenesses of objects shows an affinity with the glass botanical models in the Harvard Museum of Natural History, but rubbing up against these antiquated scientific models is also the science fiction dream of cloning.

If more recent art history would associate the act of copying with the Pictures Generation's appropriation of mass-produced images, another historical arc that insinuates itself in Sietsema's artwork is the role of transcription. The act of copying propels historical models into future discourse, ensuring the traffic of ideas as a renewable resource. Ultimately, the artist suspends his fabricated artifacts in the ethereal light of projection in order to map out historical conventions that are as constructed as the film loop. The slow march of these images across long takes and static framing is anchored to an extensive physical archive of sculpted objects, which in turn generate their own status as unwitting ethnographic fragments, fragile remains of the artistic voyage.

Sietsema's appropriations are an elaborate melding of then and now in a simultaneous capture. The film *Anticultural Positions* (2009) illustrates this strategy by using the voice of an artistic forebear to stand in as his own on the occasion of a lecture invitation at The New School in New York. On February 23, 2009, eschewing the expected PowerPoint presentation, Sietsema instead offered a silent film. In so doing, he chose to enact the concerns of his practice rather than reduce them to bullet-point digest form. The film's title is borrowed from a lecture delivered by Jean Dubuffet at the Arts Club of Chicago in 1951, but the words are derived from thoughts expressed in a 1952 essay by Dubuffet evocatively titled "Landscaped Tables,

Landscapes of the Mind, Stones of Philosophy."[1] Sietsema takes the words and slightly tweaks them to arrive at his own artist's statement. The cadence of the phrasing suggests the age of the text, yet all the descriptors mix uncannily with the images present in the film, creating an echo. Comparing the original record and the derivative, we find a pair of fraternal twins:

Dubuffet:

"The so interesting mental processes of a man undertaking to paint things and to create life, mysteriously, with his hands—a sort of life to the square root—will be all the more enlightening, I think, if the presence of the painter (and that of his hands) manifests itself more visibly in the work."[2]

Sietsema:

"The so interesting mental process of undertaking to describe things and to create life, mysteriously, with one's hands is all the more enlightening, I think, if the presence of the maker manifests itself more visibly in the work."

The alteration is subtle in this transposition of one artist's subjectivity for another. In the slight variance, Sietsema reclassifies his own activity as a form of "describing things," aligning the impulse to make work with a taxonomic drive. He also updates the source by employing the non-gendered subject "the maker" in place of the older dominant categories "man" and "painter." What is preserved, however, is the notion of presence, an artistic trope largely rejected by the interceding generation of 1960s Conceptual artists to which Sietsema is also indebted. To complicate the affinities, Sietsema's chosen medium is a mechanical process, one that has been accused of annexing the aura of the artwork.

The words extricated from Dubuffet run along the lower edge of the frame, printed like subtitles on black leader and interspersed with negative shots of Sietsema's studio worktables. Stains, drips, surface scratches, and material accretions conspire to create a landscape—a terrain vague of accidental abstract gesture—that

---

1. Jean Dubuffet, "Landscaped Tables, Landscapes of the Mind, Stones of Philosophy" (New York: Pierre Matisse Gallery, 1952), reprinted in the exhibition catalogue *Jean Dubuffet: Retrospective* (Dallas: Dallas Museum of Fine Arts and Counterpoint Press, 1966).
2. Ibid.

is strangely illustrative of the text. Debris of drawing and other forms of fabrication overwrite one another on the table's surface in a palimpsest of the artist's pursuits. The logic of sympathetic magic imposes itself in the marriage of the words and images, and the grain of the film, with its crystalline understructure, finds an affinity in Dubuffet's use of sand to texture his paintings. Amid the abstraction, a readable signifier appears: the logo mark of the United States Postal Service, and with it, the suggestion of an envoy, an exchange, a correspondence.

Sietsema's films often take the guise of missives. *Telegraph* (2012), for instance, features wood shards arranged into rough letterforms. The sticks are scavenged both from the vicinity of the artist's studio (the site implicated in all of his films) and from New Orleans after it was ravaged by Hurricane Katrina. The resulting primal glyphs are strung together through a series of cuts and fadeouts to spell "L/E/T/T/E/R/T/O/A/Y/O/U/N/G/P/A/I/N/T/E/R." The reading process in the film is stopped down in a way that highlights the physical material and its sculptural arrangement over its legibility. We stumble through these letters in an attempt to synthesize the content. Through this fog, the act of reading is brought into closer scrutiny and slowed to a point incongruous with the usual instantaneous visual intake of information culture.

The film also alludes to a specialist's conversation, the ongoing dialogue between artists through time, exemplified by the literary precedent of Rainer Maria Rilke's *Letter to a Young Poet*. The addressee of Sietsema's film, however, is an artist who died prematurely in the 1970s, and thus the film reaches back in time only to access a future curtailed. The reading process, by definition, involves downtime between composition and receipt, which is perfectly diagrammed in *Telegraph*. All texts fall into moments of interphase; they lay dormant until new meaning is assigned in concert with the active present of their reception. Artistic production is to this day moored to this same dialectic of constitution and circulation, falling in and out of currency with the imperatives of current taste, sentiment, and perception. Sietsema is interested in highlighting the entanglement of objects in historical trappings, allowing that their signification is a permutable casing.

At the hour of tea (2013) is a film in which objects live outside of time. Like *Telegraph*, it is notable for its inclusion of found material over artist-built objects within the frame. The objects in *At the hour of tea* are assembled with the calculated care of window displays in the Parisian arcades, which is also to say, following the art historical convention of the still life. In place of ripe fruit, the subjects are outdated objects: a typewriter, some expired currency, a stopped pocket watch, pages of an out-of-print magazine, a paper calendar, a crystal goblet, and a typed letter. Sietsema meshes different eras through transpositions that confirm a time-traveler's sensibility. For example, the calendar, though appearing of 1920s design, shows the date Tuesday, February 26, 2013. The title *At the hour of tea* is also a temporal graft, a phrase gleaned from a 1929 issue of *Femina* magazine conjuring a special category of leisure time. The U.S. currency in the film (also printed in 1929) is by contrast still legal tender, readily tradable for contemporary consumer goods.

The difference between the paper bills and magazine pages highlights the accrual of value in collector goods versus the value of objects still in circulation. Another important object of confused provenance in *At the hour of tea* is an exhibition catalogue of Art Deco design that bears the artist's name, the name of a deceased art historian, and a recent publication date. Here, again, the artist's subjectivity is allowed to float freely in time, in this instance showing the seal of approval of a little-known German critic. The cover is modeled on a Leipzig imprint devoted to charting the new art of that day. By inserting himself in this frame as the proverbial young artist, Sietsema creates an impossible juxtaposition of progress and retroactivity, invoking a dead critic to explicate his own latest output. Beyond the critical approval suggested by the invented monograph, artistic legitimacy is also signaled by a commercial seal: the letterhead of Matthew Marks Gallery embossed with the impression of a Roman coin bearing a helmeted head of Mars (the ancient Roman root of the name Marks). This invented overlay superimposes one type of official currency with another, one empire for another.

Within the complicated structures of market acceptance, the role of the critic in conferring a place in history is also a tension Sietsema recurrently explores. *The sentence* (2012) takes special aim at the artist-critic dyad through a phrase redeployed from Benjamin Franklin's essay "Advice to a Young Tradesman, Written by an Old One."[3]

---

3. Benjamin Franklin, "Advice to a Young Tradesman, Written by an Old One," July 21, 1748, originally published in George Fisher, *The American Instructor: or Young Man's Best Companion*, ninth edition (Philadelphia: B. Franklin and D. Hall, 1748) and reprinted in *Lapham's Quarterly*, Spring 2008.

Substituting "critic" for "creditor" and "quill and well" for "money," Sietsema recasts the sentence as:

"The/Sound/of/your/hammer/at/Five/in/the/Morning/or/Nine/ at/Night/heard/by/a Critic/makes/him/easy/Six/Months/longer/ But/if he/sees/you/at/a/Billiard/Table or/hears/your/Voice/in/a/ Tavern/when/you/should/be/at/Work/he/sends/for/his Quill/and/ Well/the/next/Day"[4]

A sentence is a grammatical unit, but it can also be a verdict, a punishment. In this particular sentence, which appears etched as in ancient tablets, the judgment of artistic integrity is chained to the demonstration of applied labor, in concord with a Protestant work ethic. This mode of appraising artworks based on their evidence of the hand of the artist runs counter to Sol LeWitt's own famous "Sentences on Conceptual Art," a set of dictums affirming that concept trumps application in an artwork. In spite of this leitmotif of the postmodern, art collectors continue to cling to the notion of hours spent in the studio, and the entry of film into the arena of art has necessitated the invention of special structures of rarity, making (inherently reproducible) films into controlled editions and encouraging a new emphasis on materiality in the moving image. At the same time, social exchange, unmoored from physical art objects, is now considered eminently collectible work. The interplay of these opposite vector economies offers a contradictory backdrop for Sietsema's process-based methods of constructing images in film.

In one of his more elaborate undertakings, Sietsema cast Clement Greenberg's apartment as the protagonist of the film *Empire* (2002). In order to represent this private abode, made public in a double-page spread of a 1964 issue of *Vogue* magazine, he sculpted a cavernous structure whose distorted proportions would match the eye of the camera, a warped vessel necessary for generating the filmic space. In order to retain the semblance of the negative on which it was shot, the film print was reattributed a red-orange hue in a formal exaggeration of the natural properties of the source. Occasionally the image flips on its horizontal axis to remind us of all the inversions that are part and parcel of the photographic process. The camera slowly pans around the room, finally becoming absorbed in a pair of red lines, the zip of a Barnett Newman painting, which

4. Ibid.

mimics the Kodak red stripe of Super 8 film, a format synonymous with the home movie.

Empire casts an image of the critic's home as a case study in the transmutations possible in the field of representation. The picture of Greenberg's apartment reads both as a record of the apex of an art movement and as a chart for the sociodynamics of a specific living space. Greenberg's widow, Jenny Van Horne, recalls that the *Vogue* fashion editor was so appalled to find visible signs of a baby inhabiting the space that she eliminated all traces of this presence in the final image. Her memory of the photo shoot confirms the degree to which the staging of a photograph can charge the narrative of its image. Like the cricket that appears camouflaged in foliage at the start of the film, Greenberg's own person is so flush with the context that he needn't even appear in person within the frame. His living room suffices to communicate his realm of influence; he vanishes into the furnishings, figure and ground collapsed. And the film folds itself over many more times, moving between the Manhattan apartment and a French Rococo interior, and transposing an artificially rendered grasshopper with a tessellated shape made by in-camera edits and superimpositions, techniques that Sietsema lifts from the tradition of avant-garde film.

At the hour of tea is also concerned with the interrelationship between figure and its surroundings. A set of directives about image composition is inscribed on a letter composed on white stationery adorned with a thick black edge, tucked into an envelope whose seams are contoured in a black X shape. This paper is a 19th-century French codification of mourning; an announcement to the reader to proceed solemnly. In photography, an X can signify either approbation—as in the grease markings on a contact sheet to indicate the selection of an image—or as negation, as in X slashes through negatives to cancel future printings. To a contemporary viewer, the X form of the envelope will also conjure the icon for email, a virtual surrogate constituted by the symbolic adaptation of the functionality of the physical envelope. The desktop in *At the hour of tea* is as stylized as the computer "desktop," with all its icons referencing the office environment. To help us complete the migration from the analog to the virtual we require transitional symbols such as the cloud, a powerful weather agent now reduced to a metaphor for data storage. This process of skeuomorphism is the toggling between the world of objects and the world of information. The buttons of graphical user interfaces—desktop, windows, and file folder icons—are grandfathering clauses meant to reassure us of a tangible world that we straddle together with the virtual.

This cohabitation of disparate eras is made comfortable under the softening cover of the film grain, and, under this veil, Sietsema courts surprising equivalencies. This easy slippage is performed to greatest effect in *Figure 3* (2008), a film in which various cultural artifacts reissued in the artist's present commingle in a joint visual field. Sculptures replicating ethnographic objects are placed in a suspension that buffers their differing geographic origins and specific attributions. Cracked, peeling, and oxidized surfaces of broken plates resemble the fissures of lunar topography. Fishing nets, traditionally made of animal gut, serve as a potent proxy for the string of film and its own capturing abilities. Amid a pileup of seemingly ancient coins, a few studio implements appear camouflaged by the same encrustation: a pair of scissors used in the editing process, a kitchen spoon used for meal breaks. Under an artificially rendered patina that conjoins these items in a shared DNA, we also find a coat check chit (a sly tool of entry for objects into the museum's collection) along with a key to access the studio, and between these two objects a line is traced between the site of artistic production and the site of preservation.

Every one of Paul Sietsema's films presents its own archaeology, the sedimentation of forms held under one skin. Sietsema sculpts images, working the film membrane as a carver polishes stone.

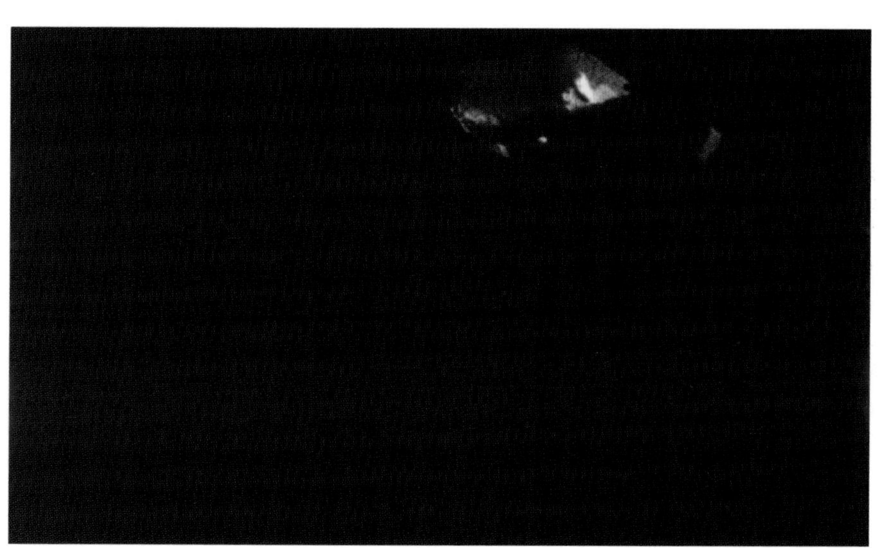

Empire, 2002

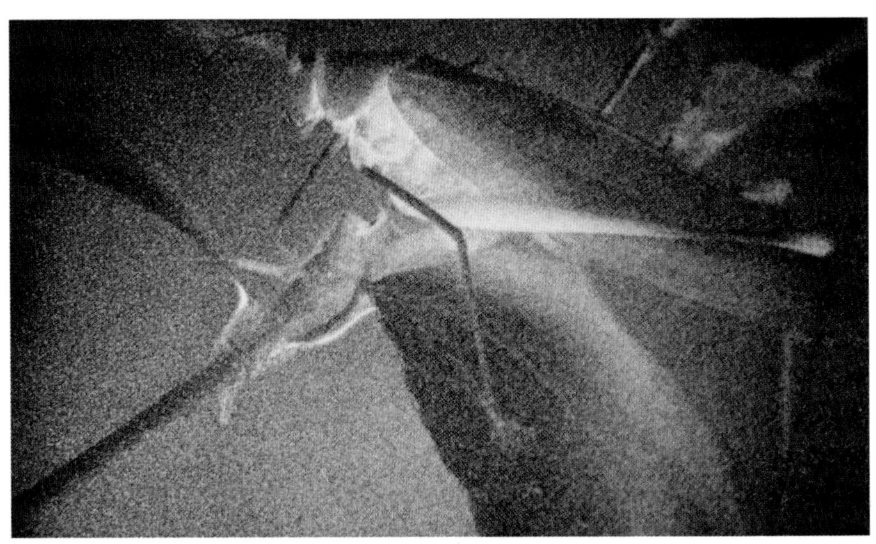

Empire

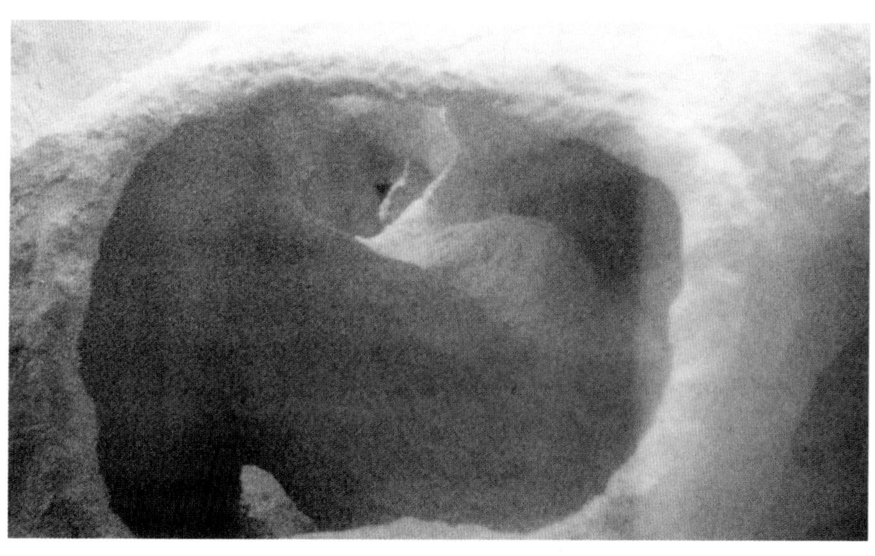

Empire

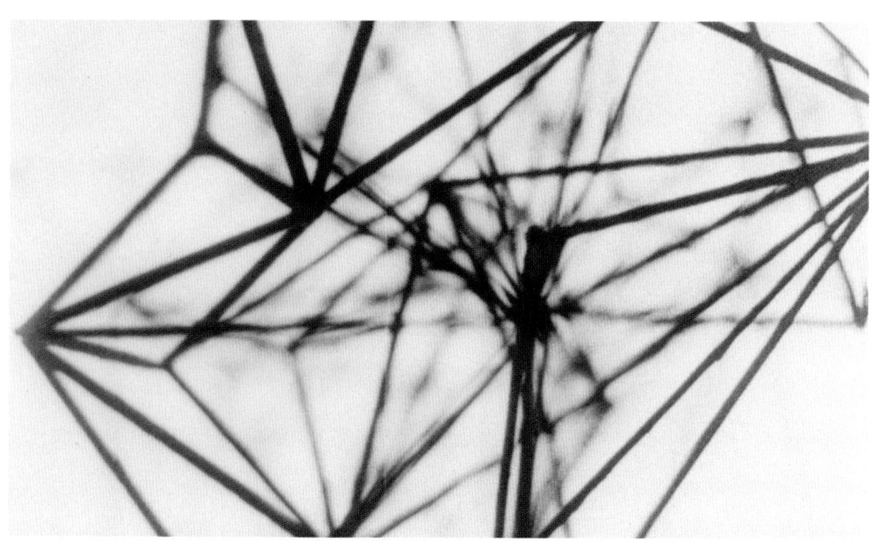

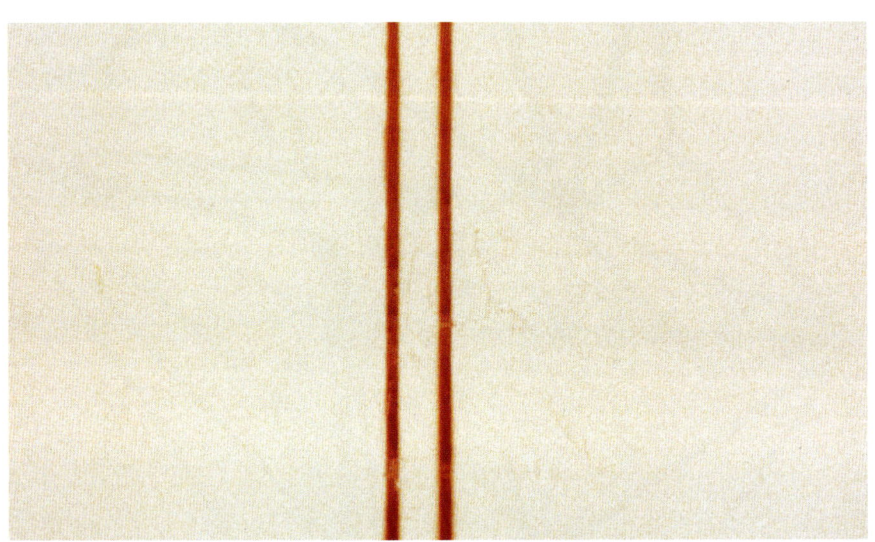

Empire

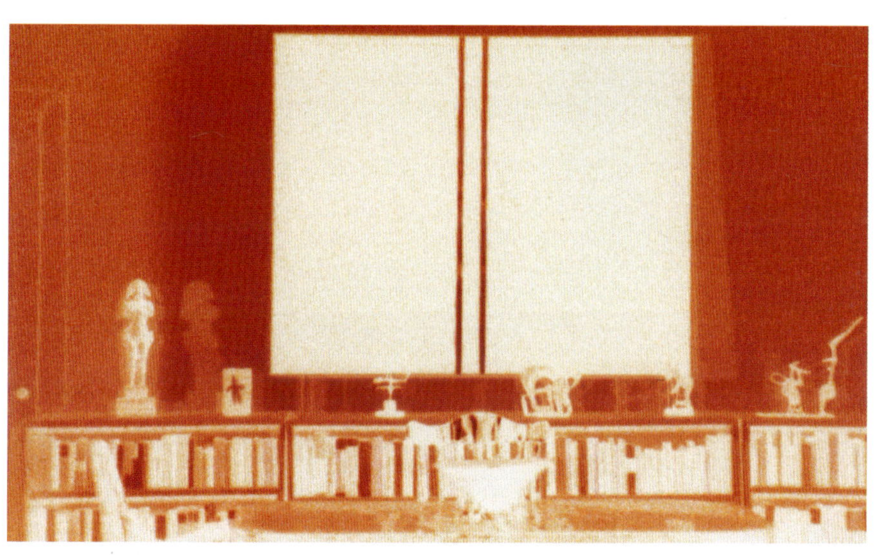

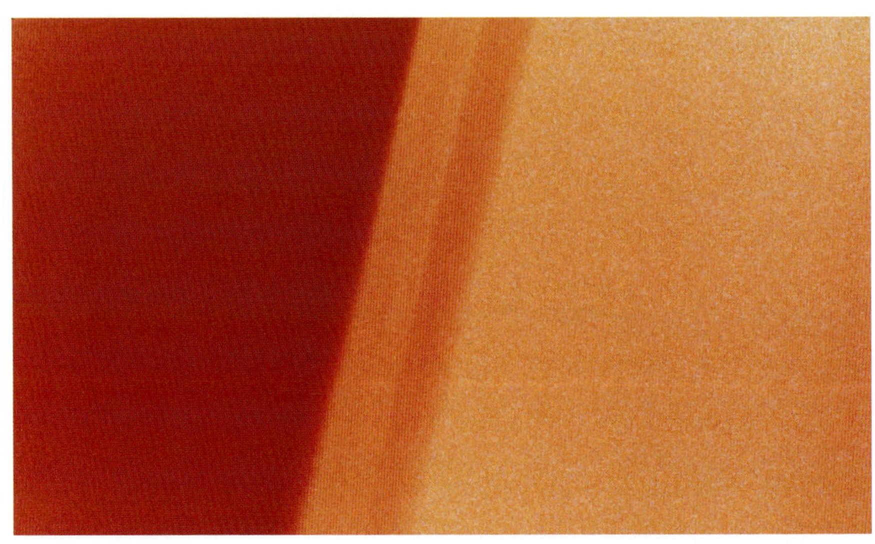

Empire

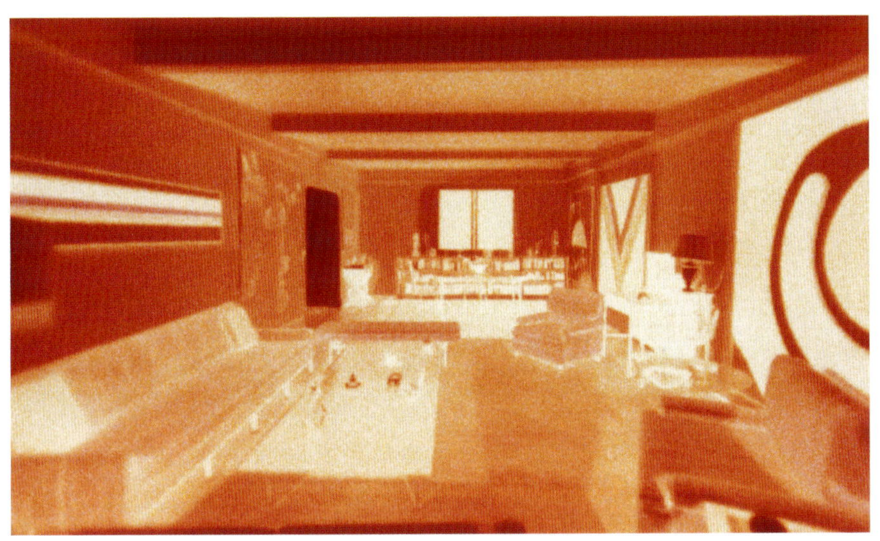

Empire

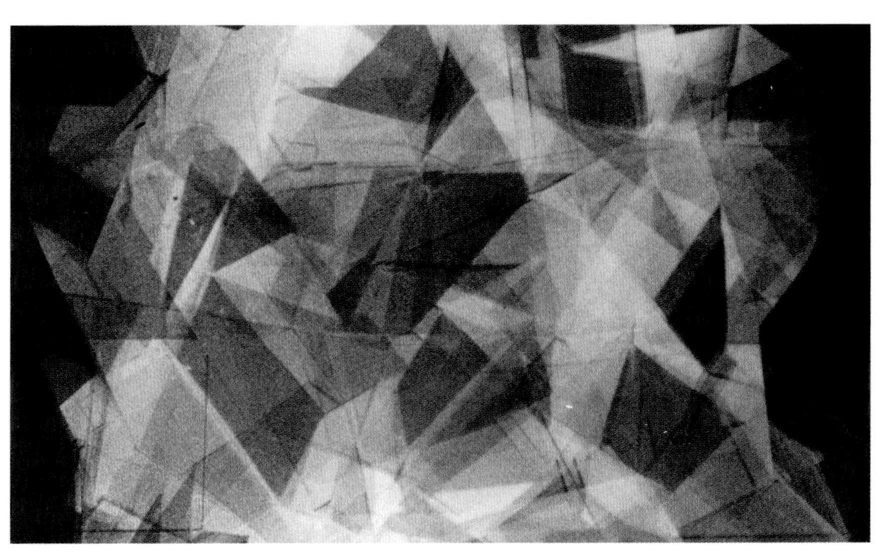

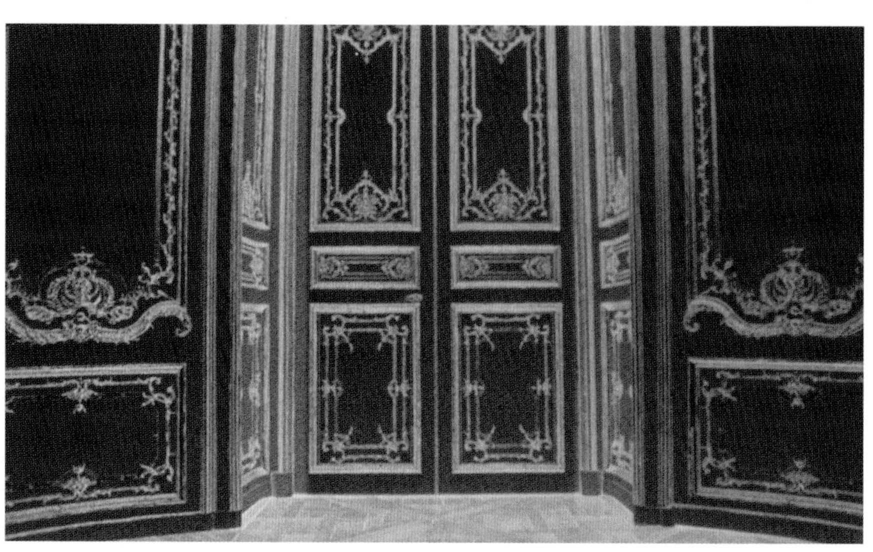

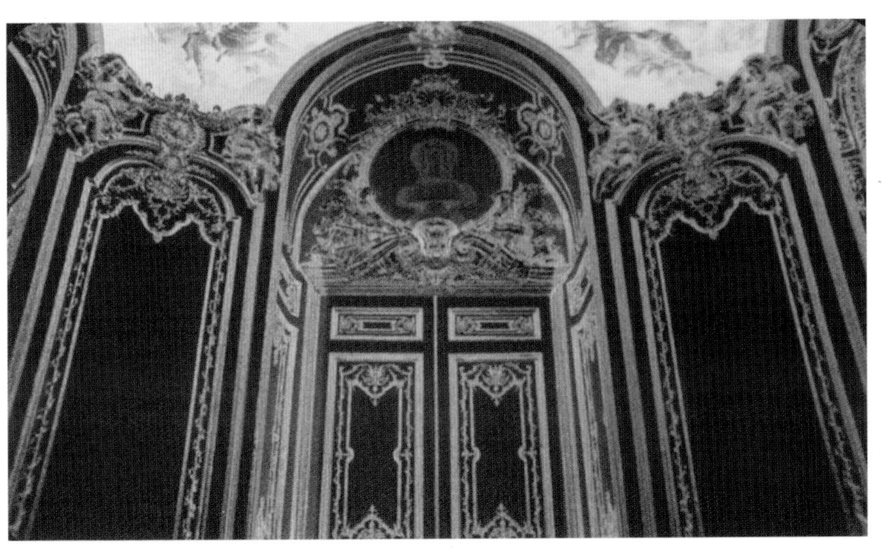

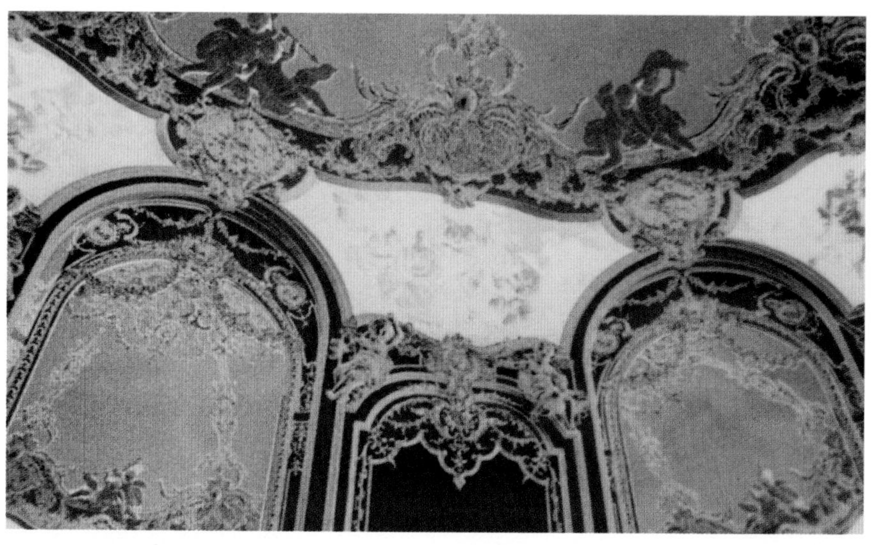

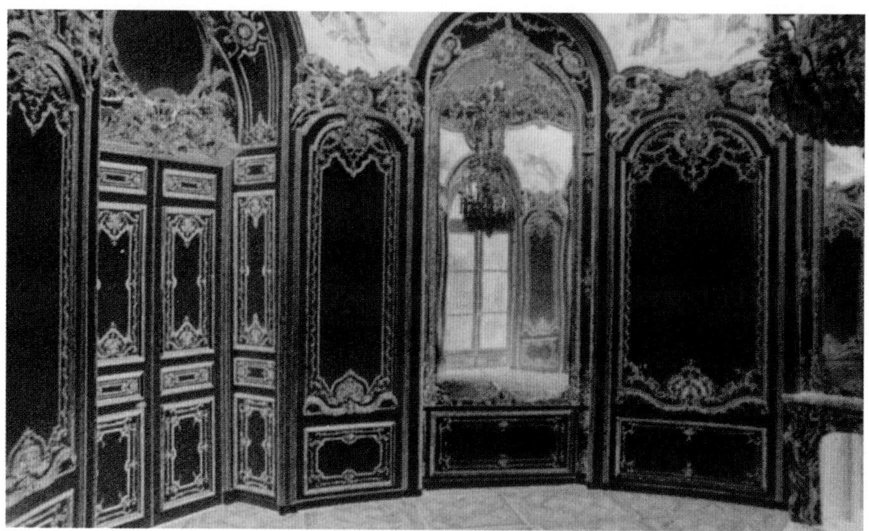

Empire

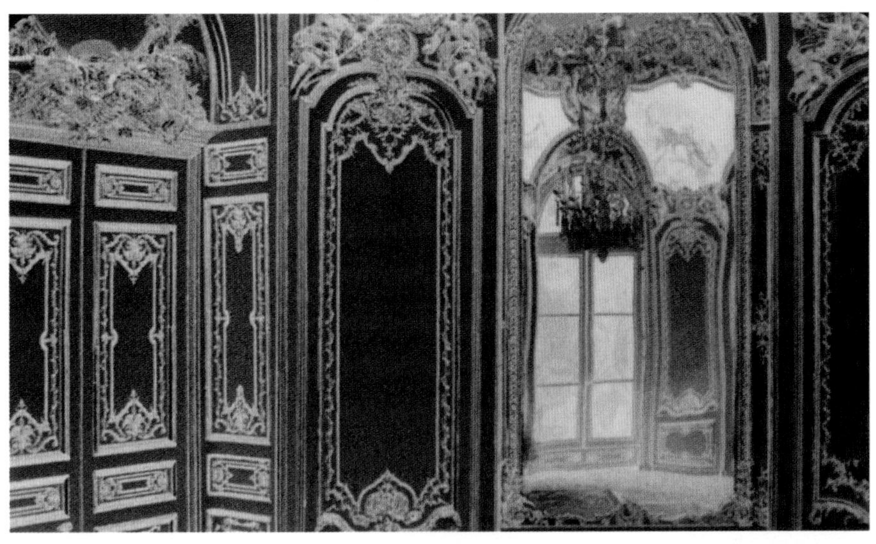

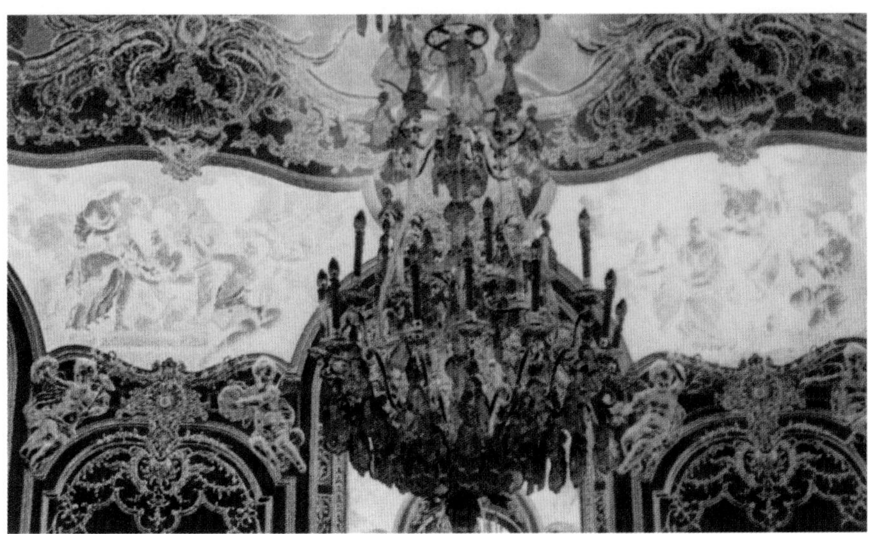

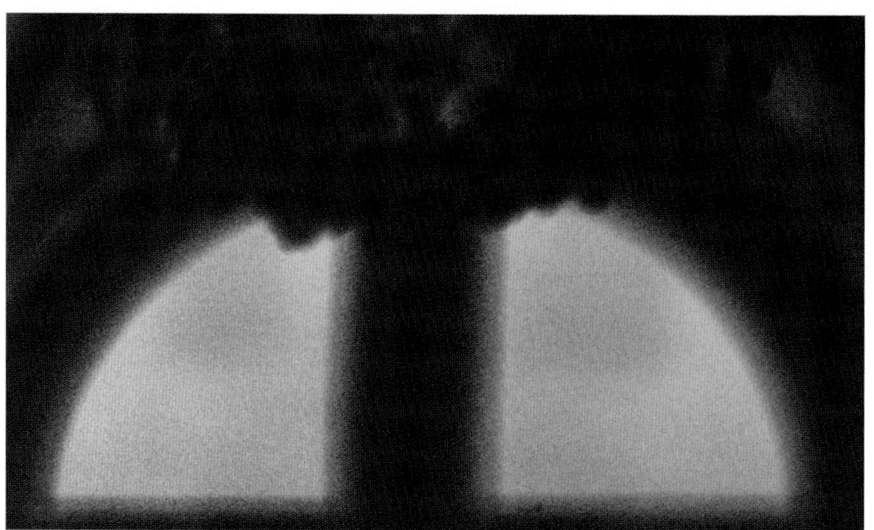

Empire

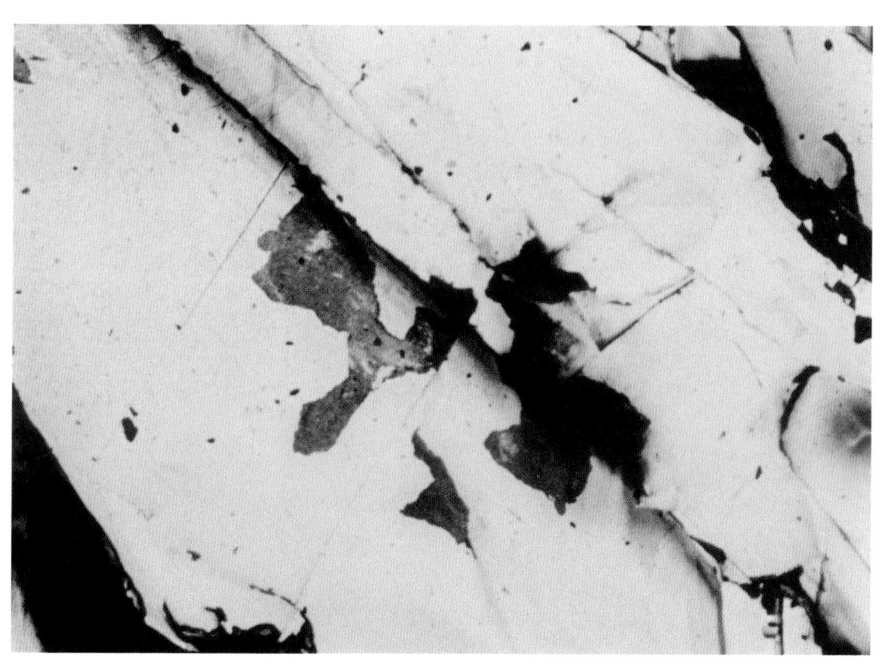

Figure 3, 2008

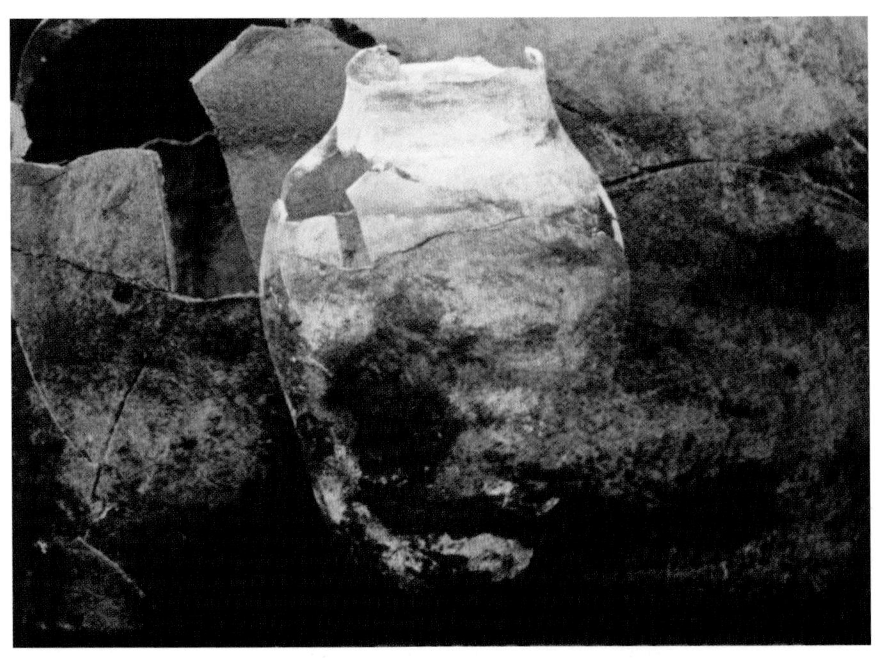

Figure 3

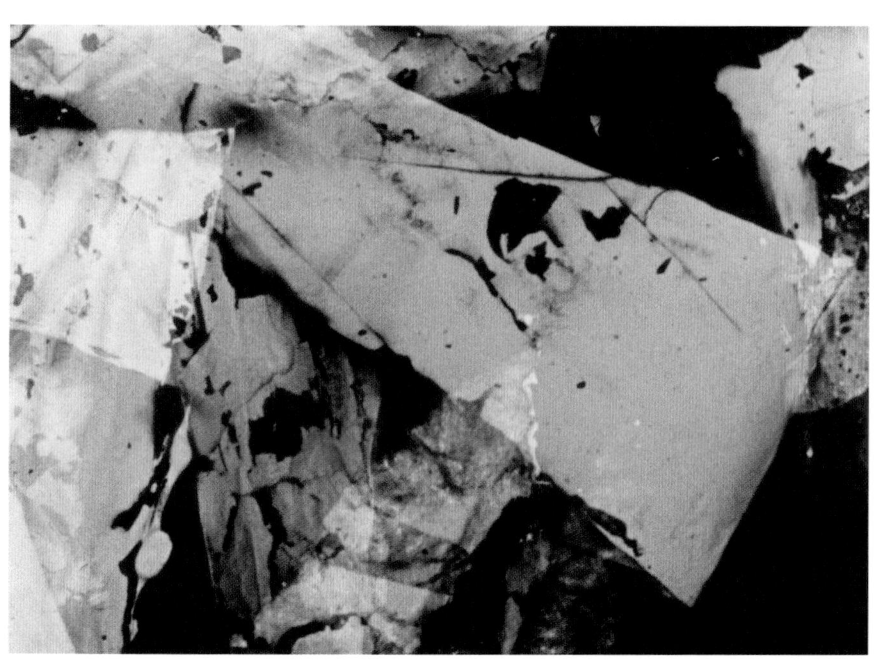

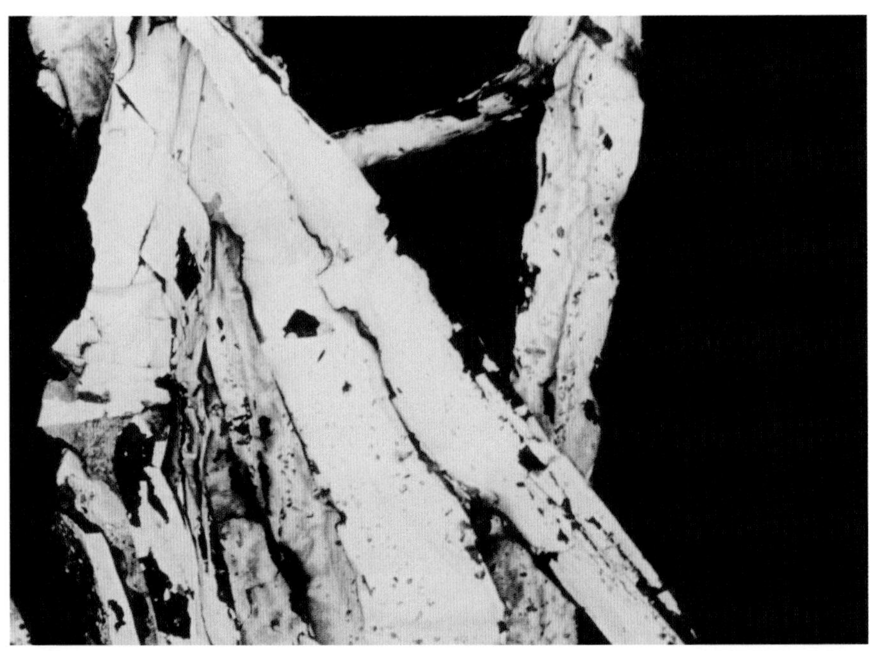

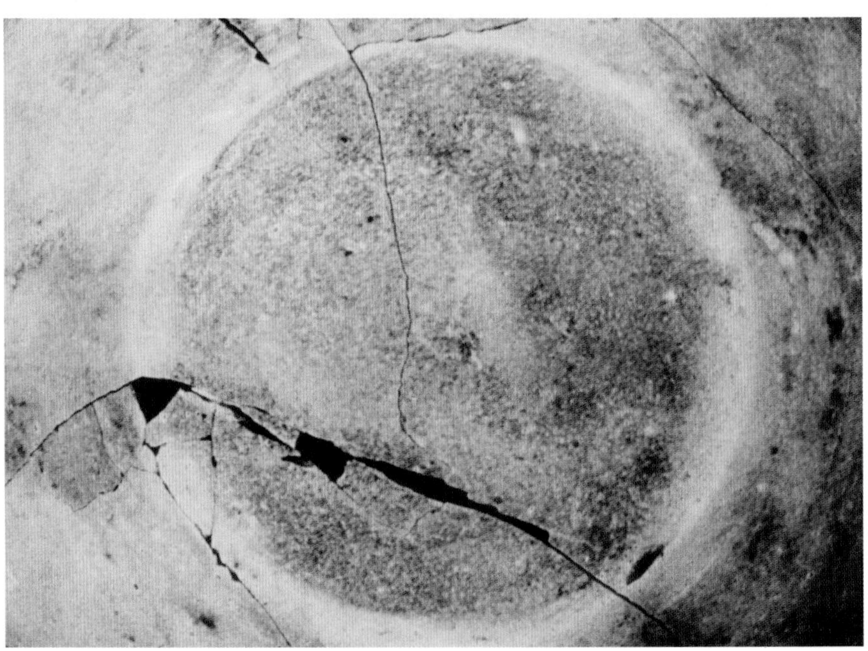

Figure 3

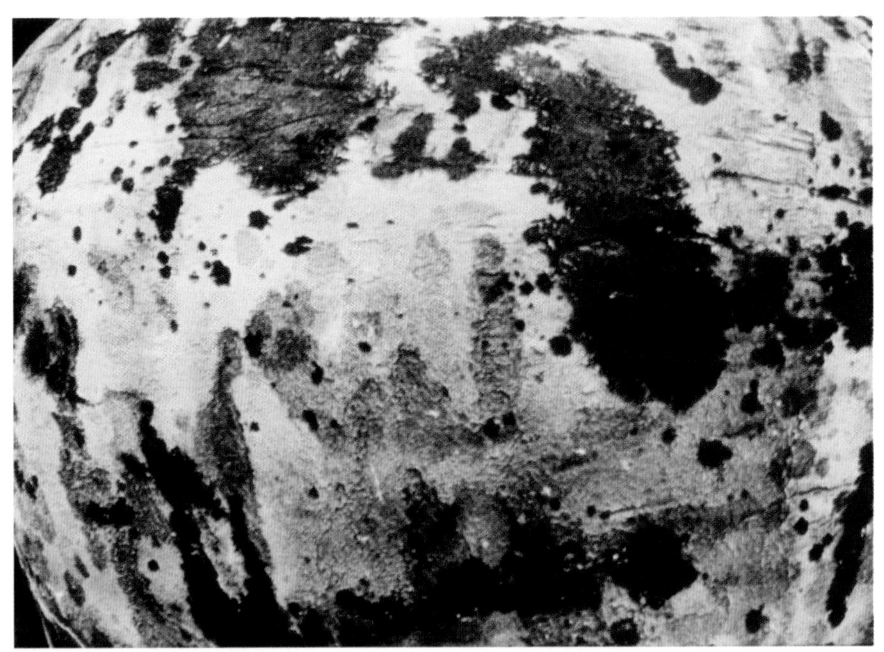

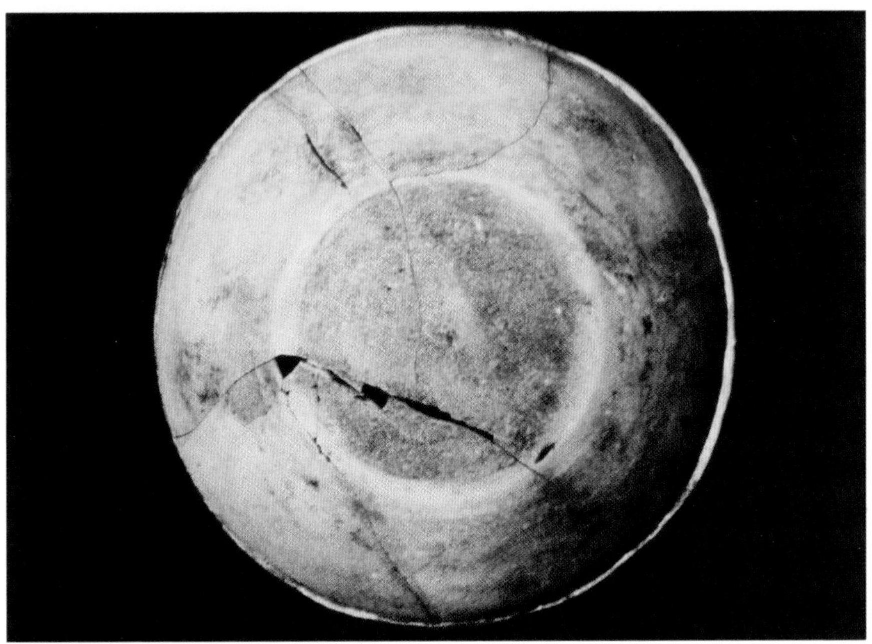

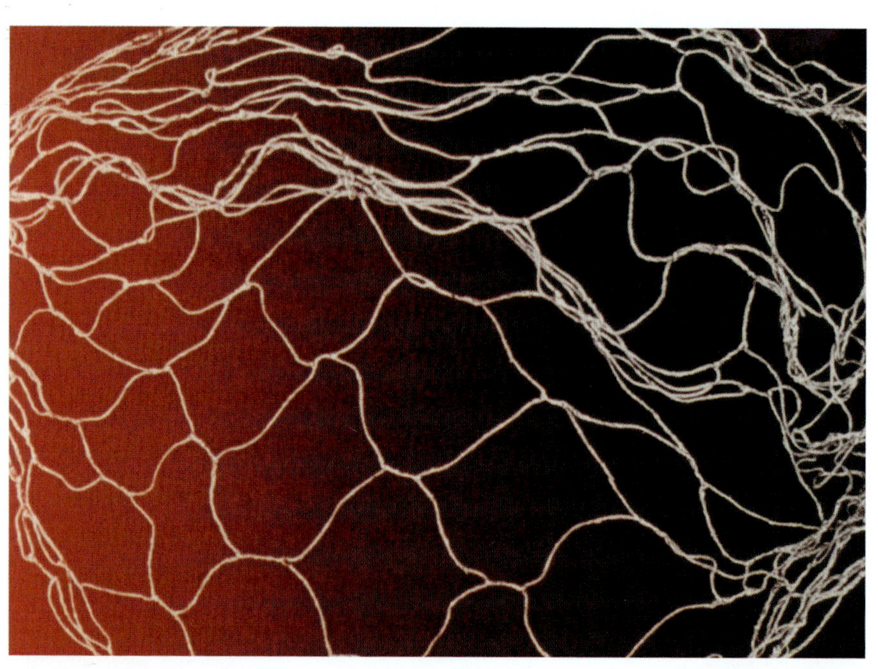

Figure 3

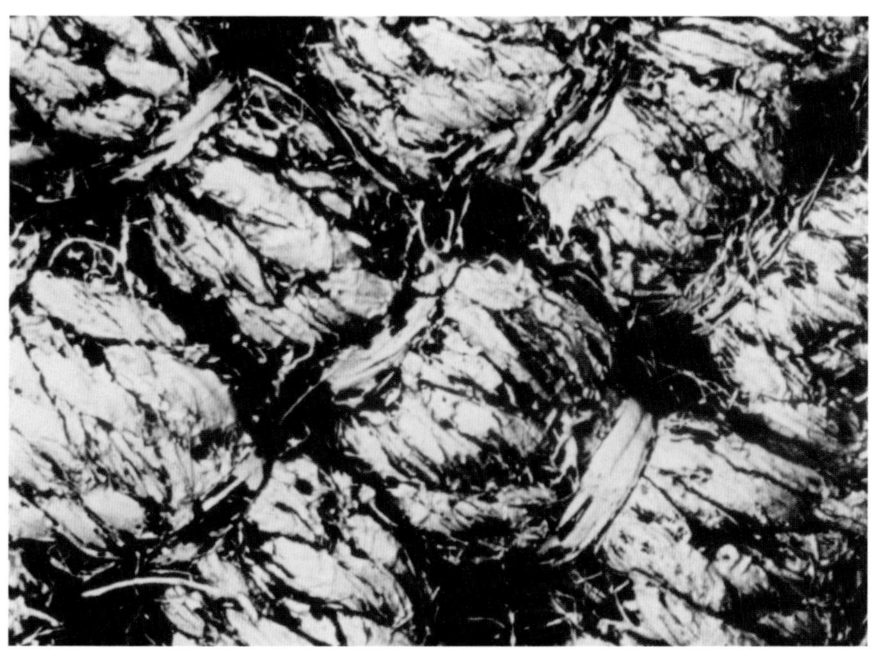

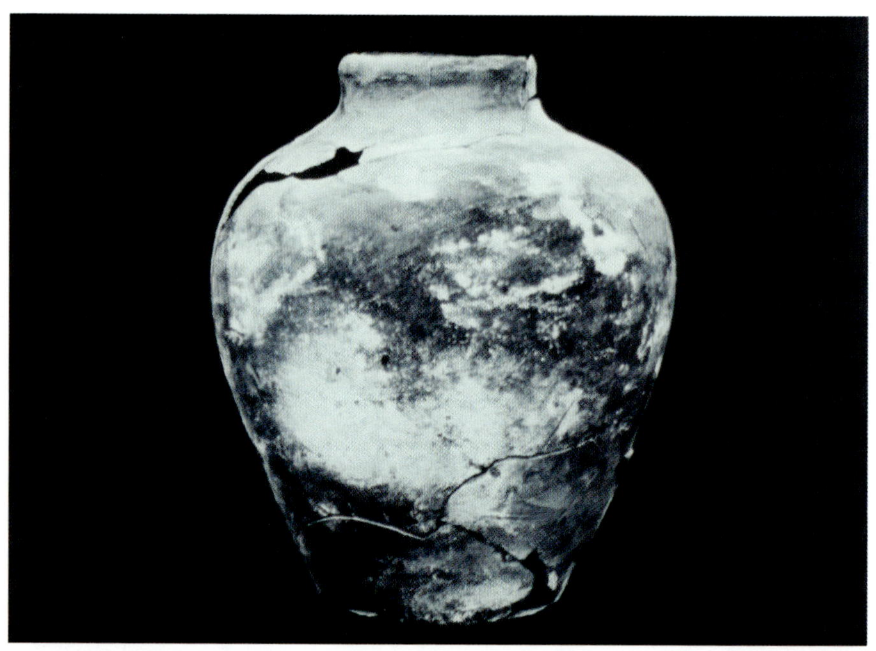

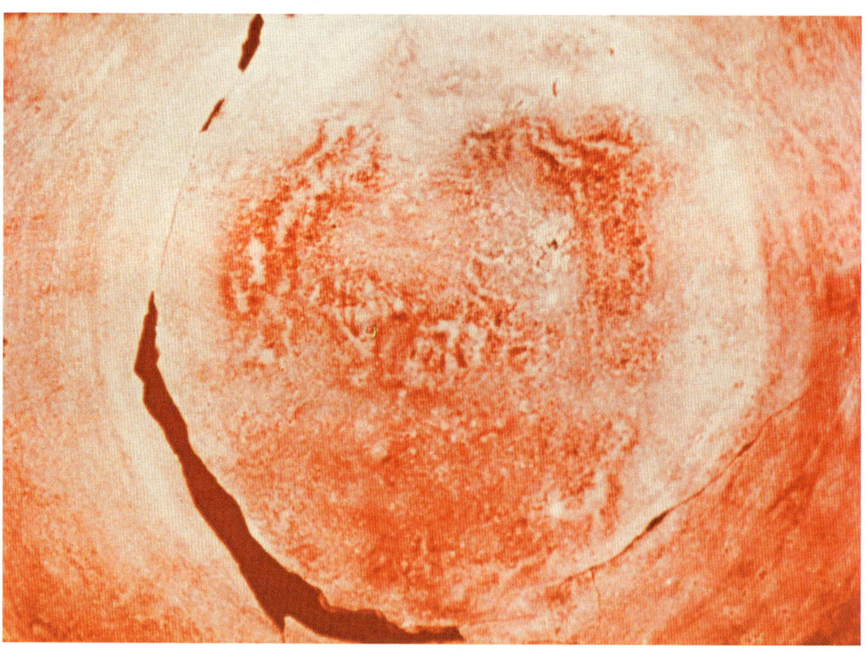

Figure 3

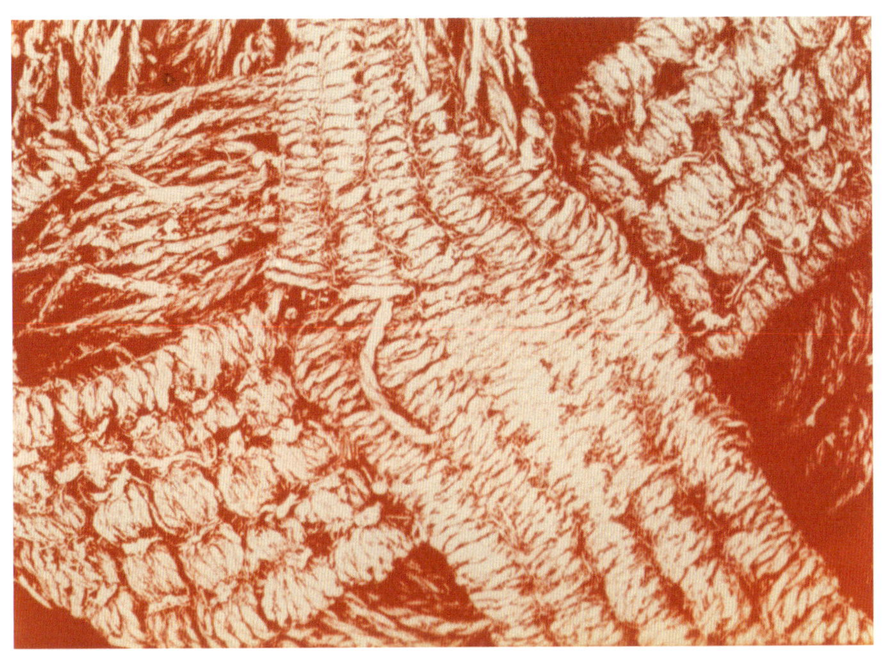

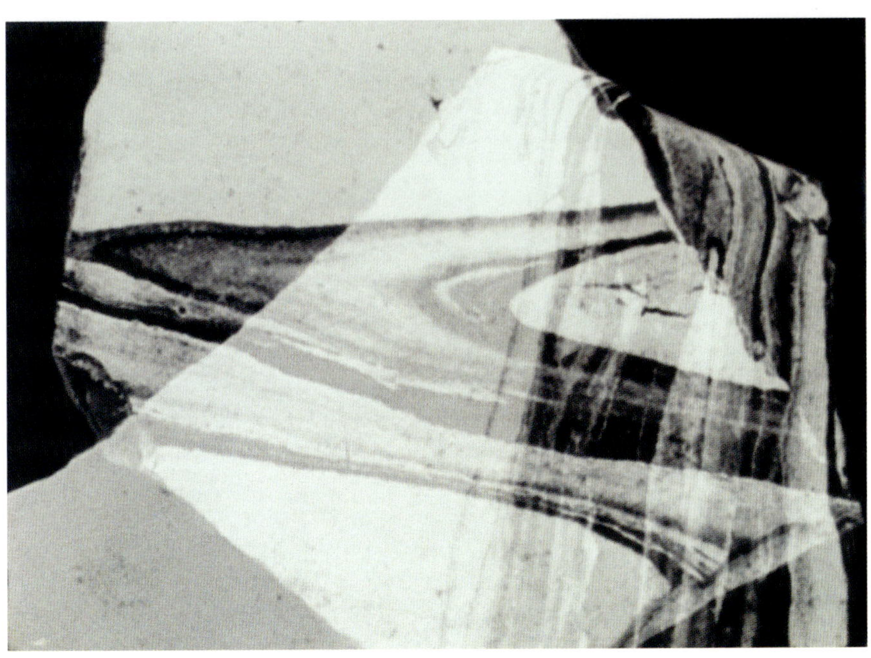

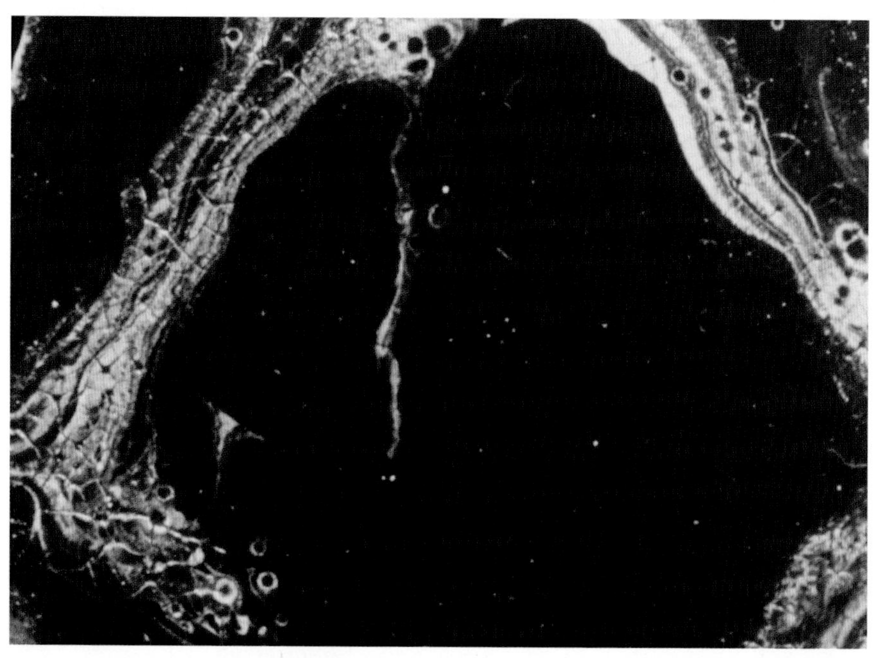

Figure 3

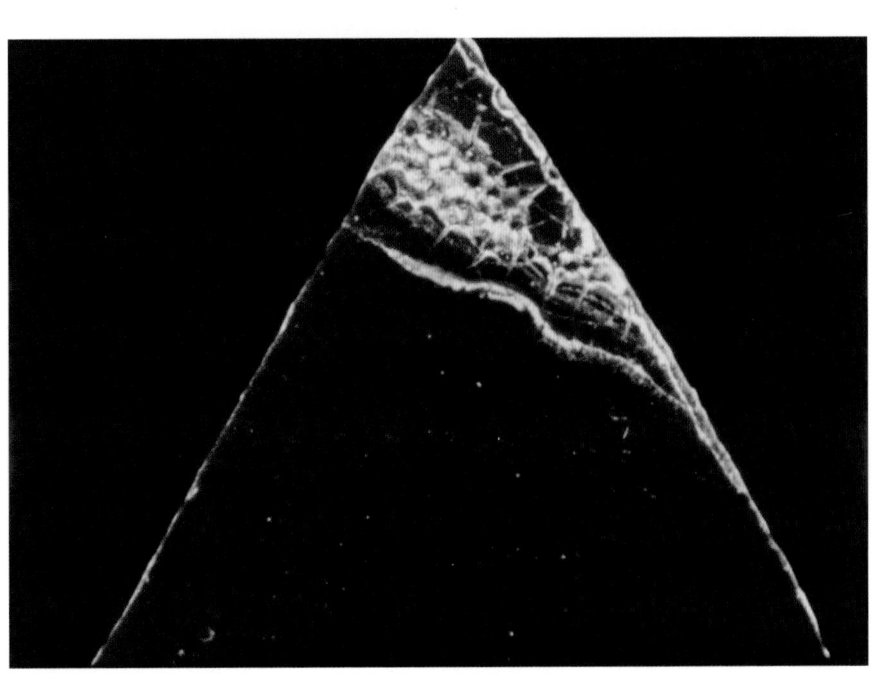

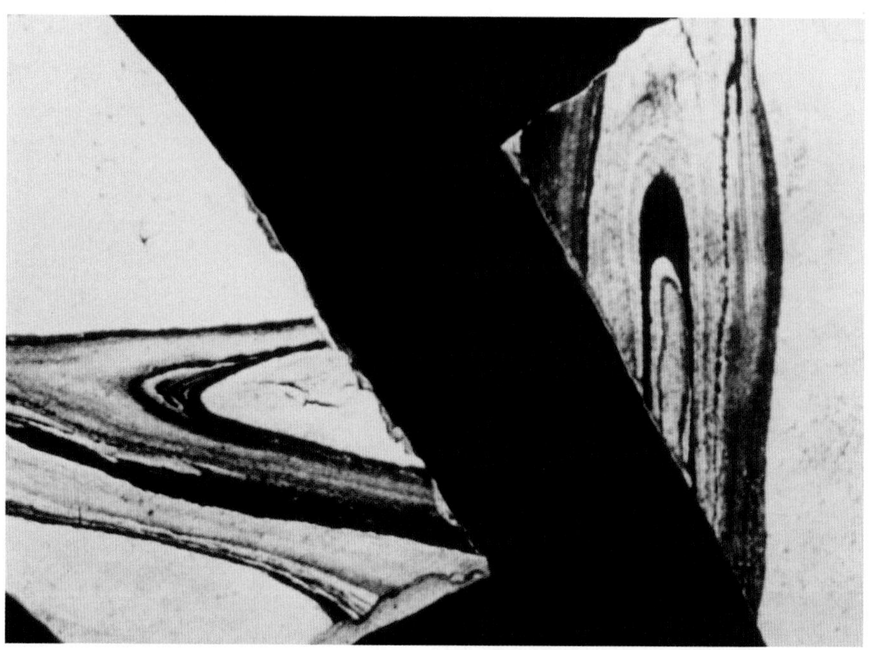

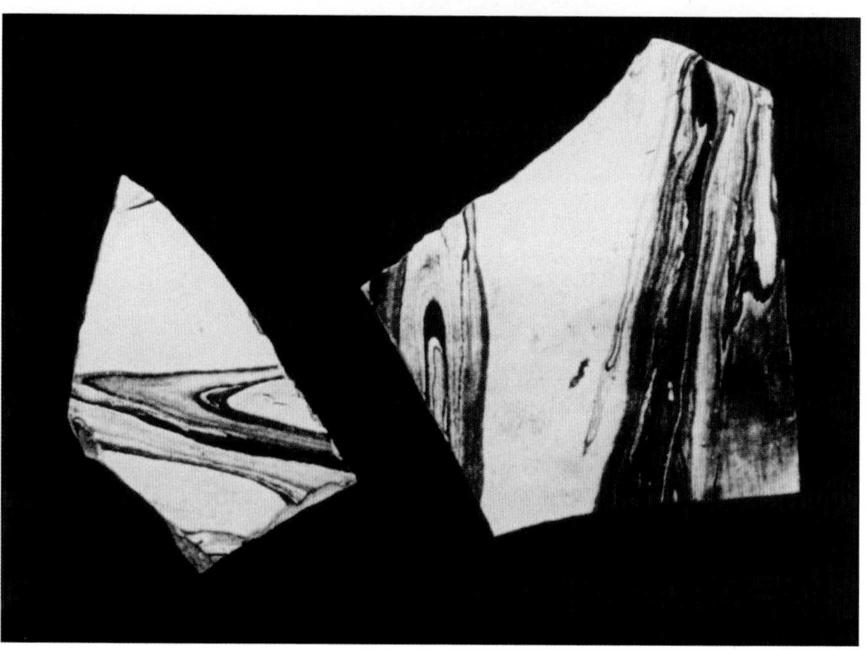

Figure 3

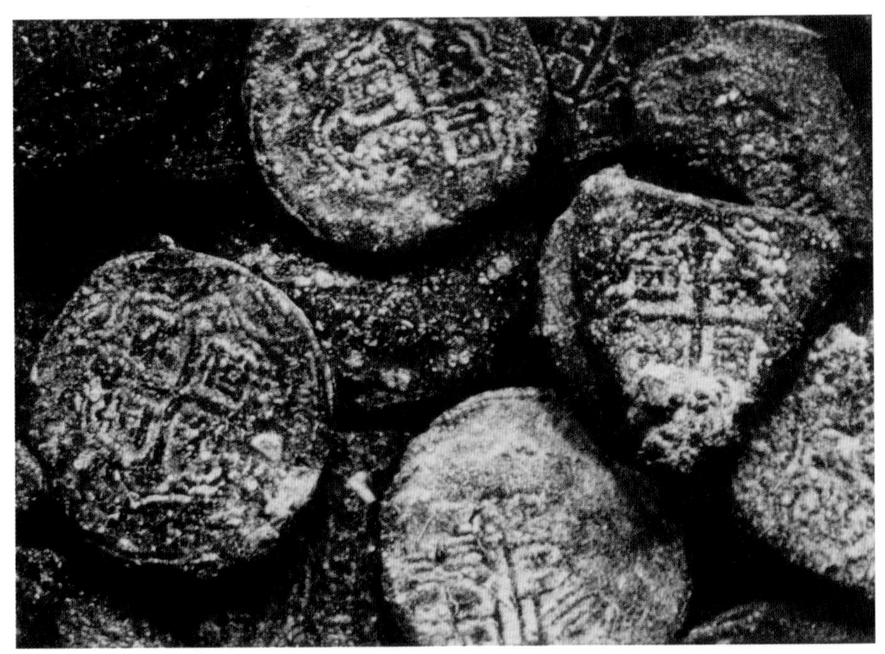

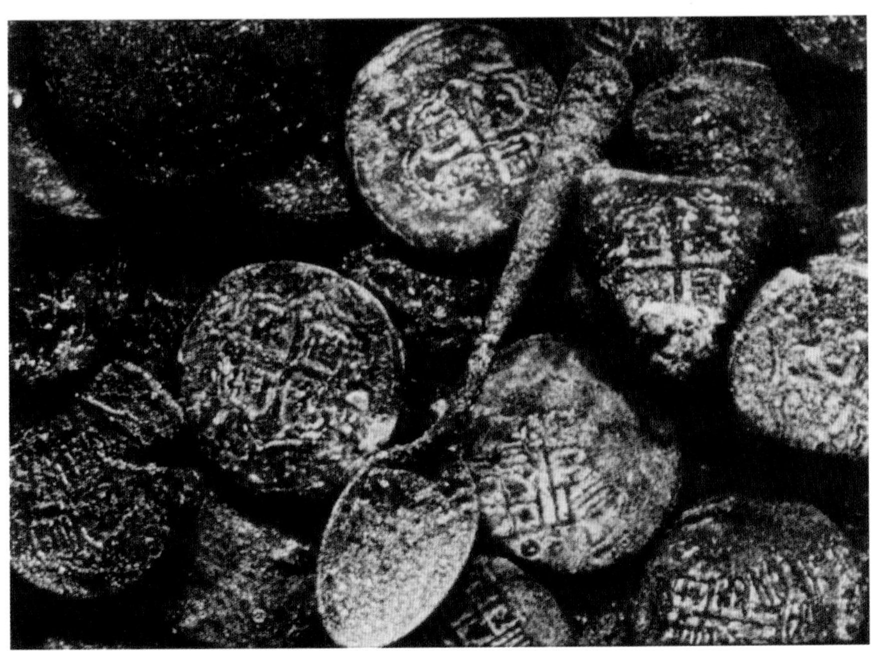

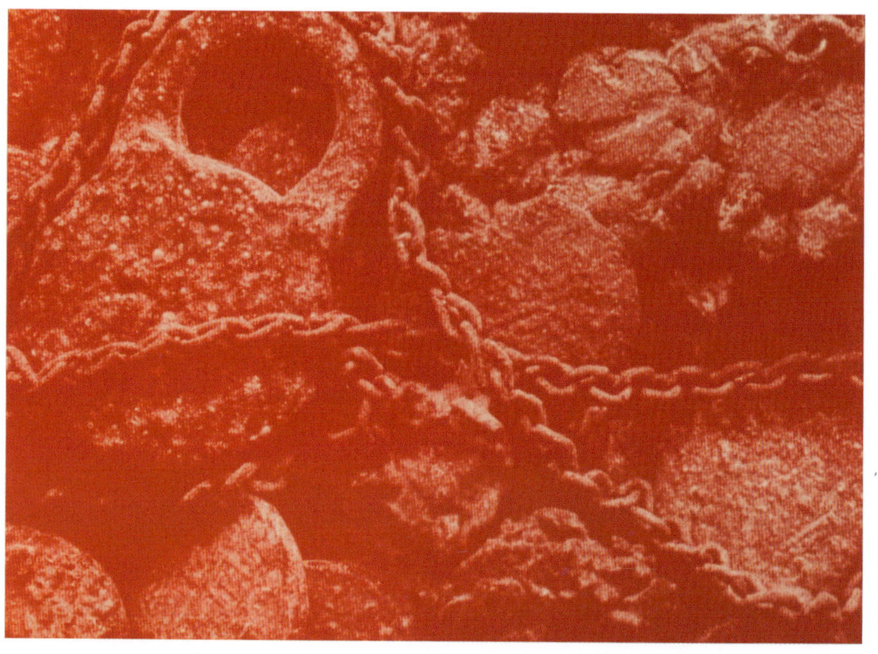

Figure 3

Anticultural Positions, 2009

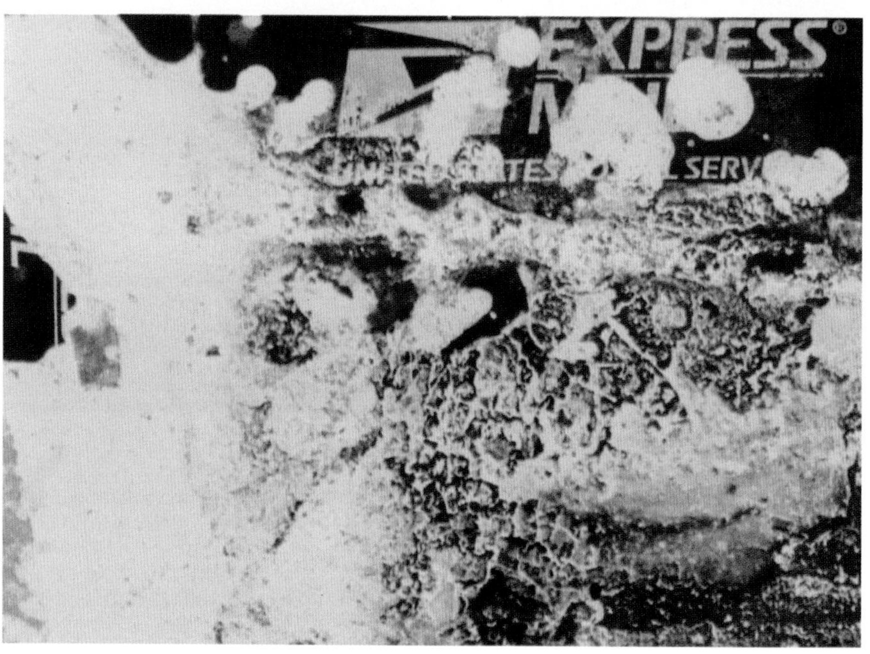

*All my works of these last years are closely linked
to the specific behavior of the material used,
and, if you will, to its disposition.*

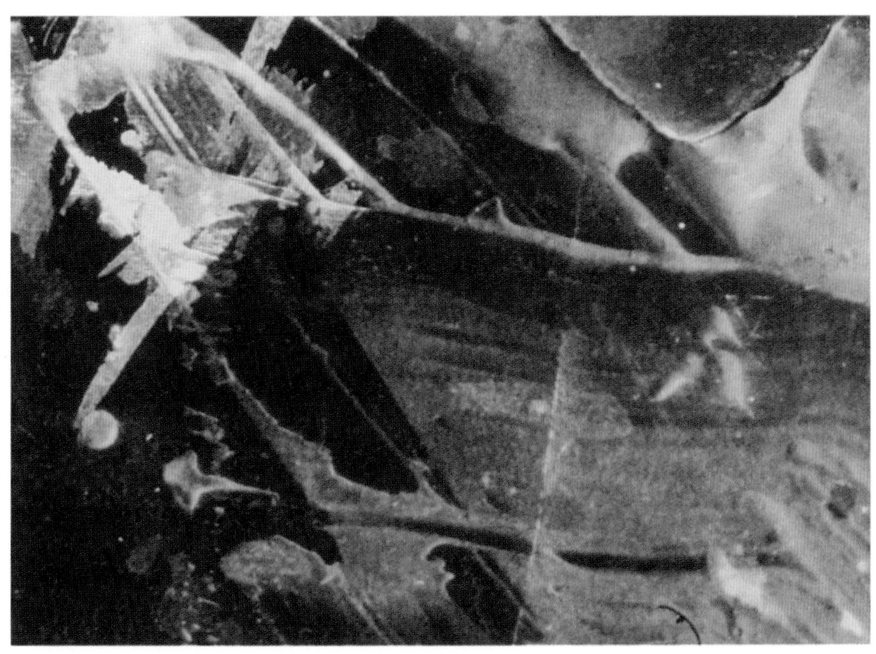

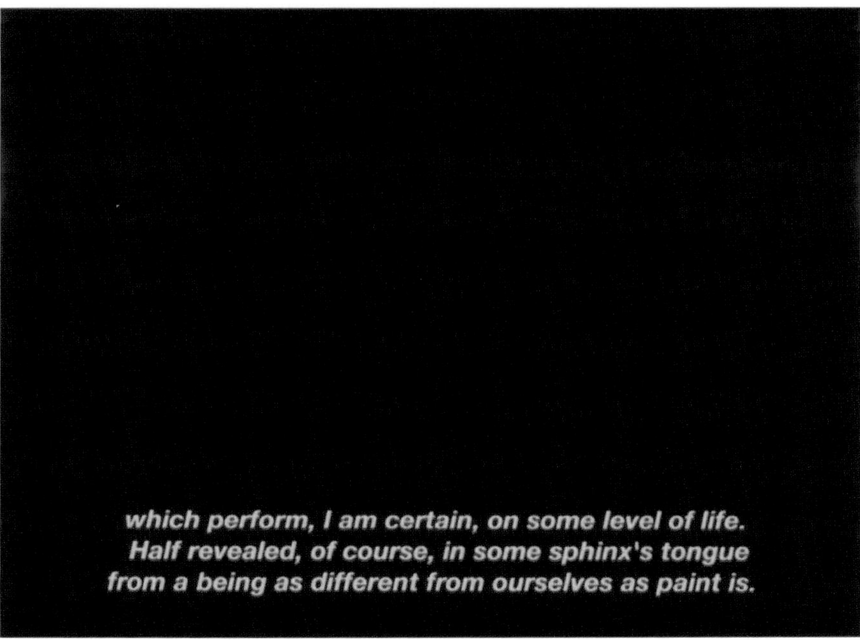
which perform, I am certain, on some level of life.
Half revealed, of course, in some sphinx's tongue
from a being as different from ourselves as paint is.

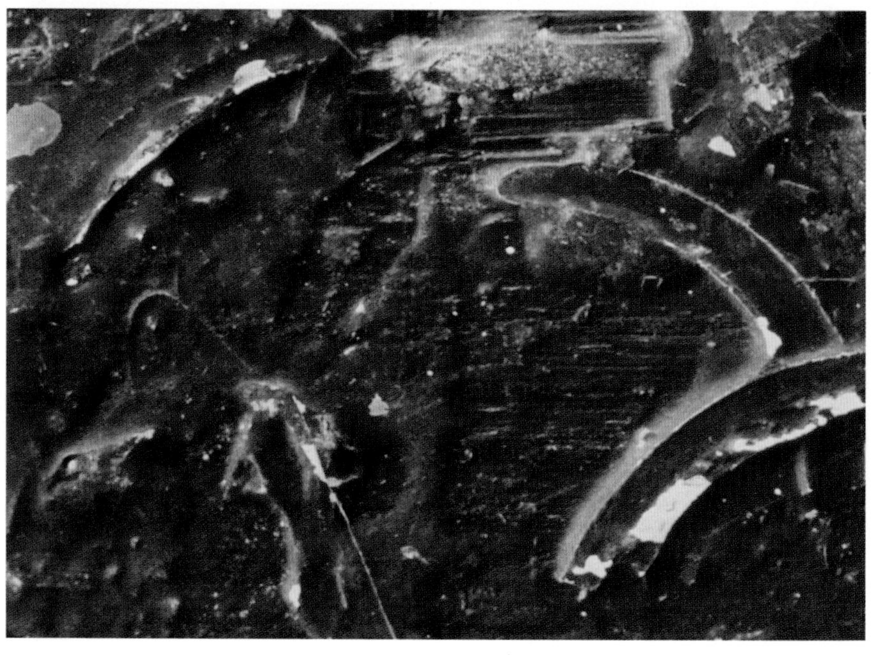

Anticultural Positions

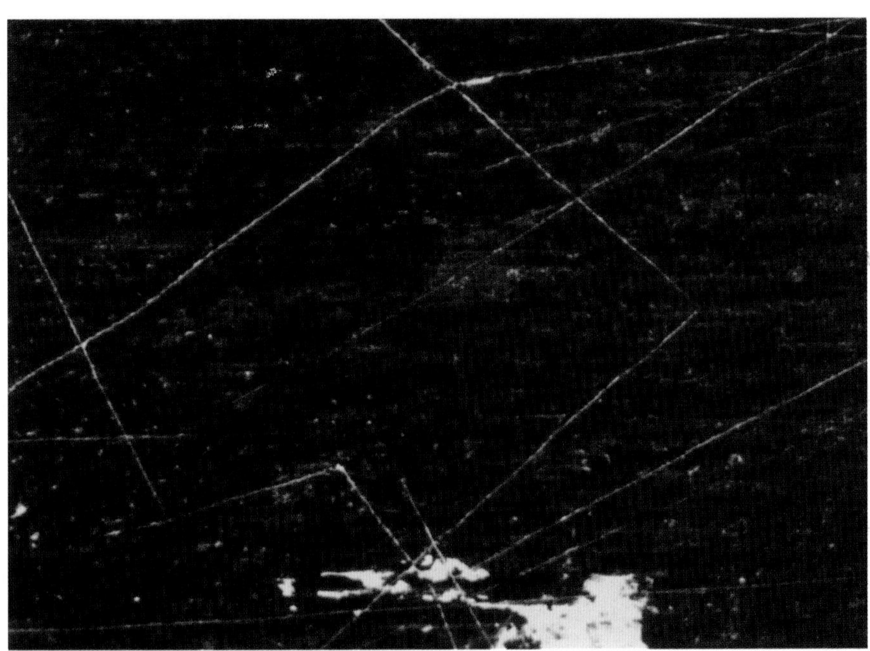

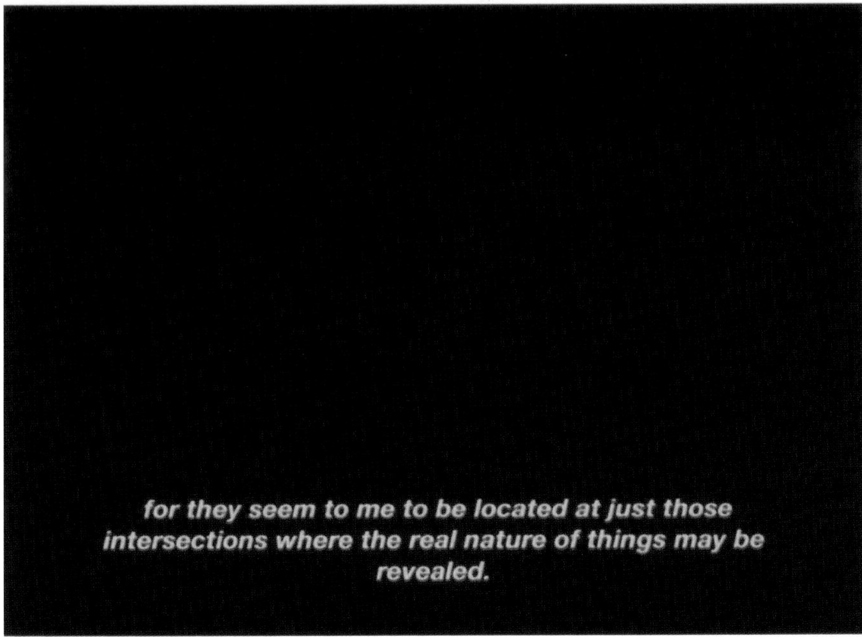
for they seem to me to be located at just those
intersections where the real nature of things may be
revealed.

Perhaps it was the time I spent in the deserts of White
Africa that sharpened my taste for the little,
the almost nothing, and, especially, in my work,

definitely outlined such as trees, roads, houses etc.,
having been eliminated.

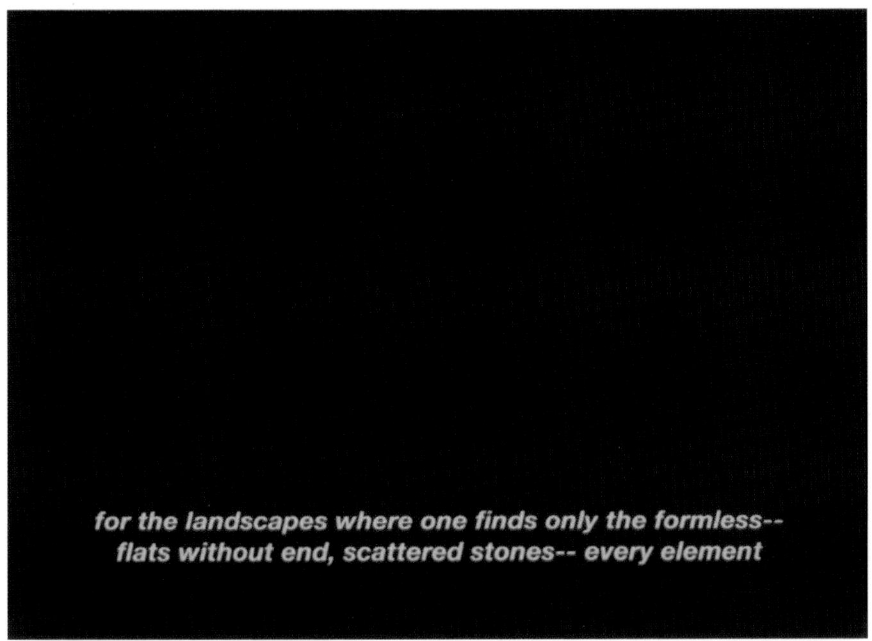
for the landscapes where one finds only the formless--
flats without end, scattered stones-- every element

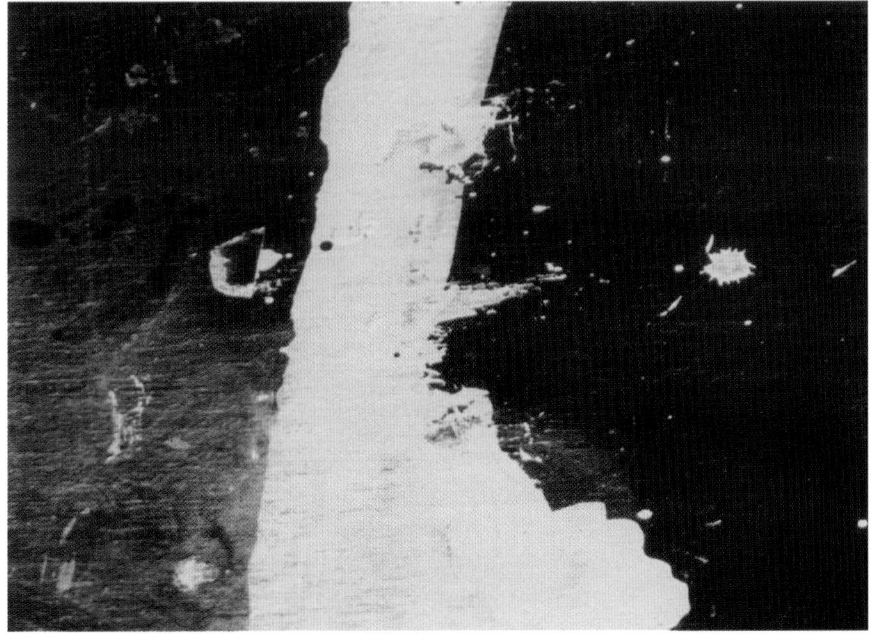

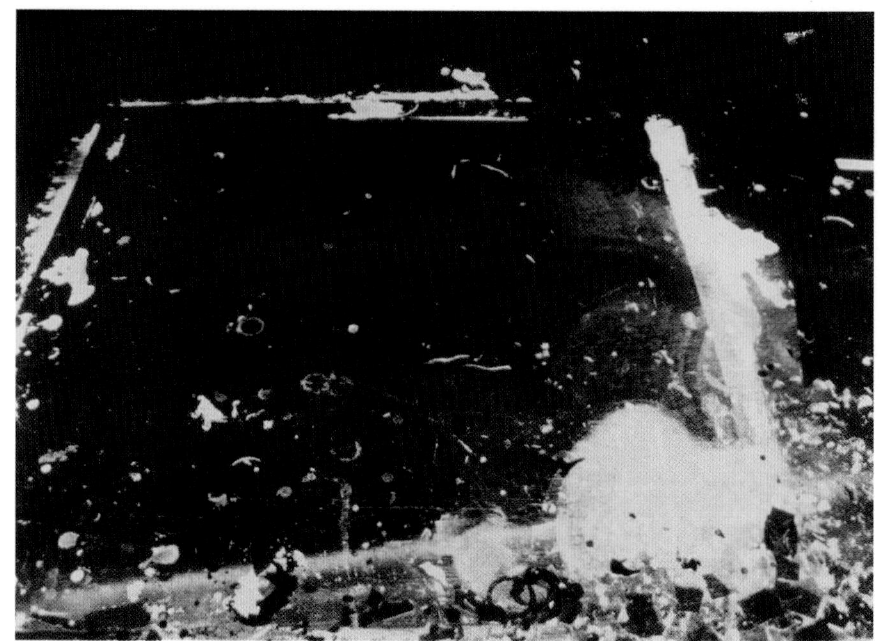

Capable of bringing to us astonishing news from
the country of the non-circumscribed,

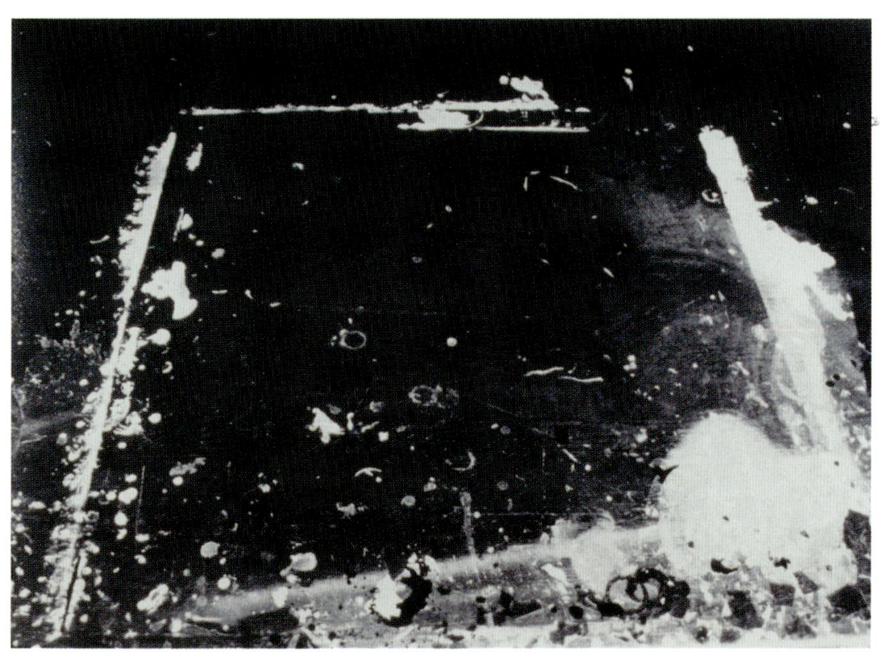

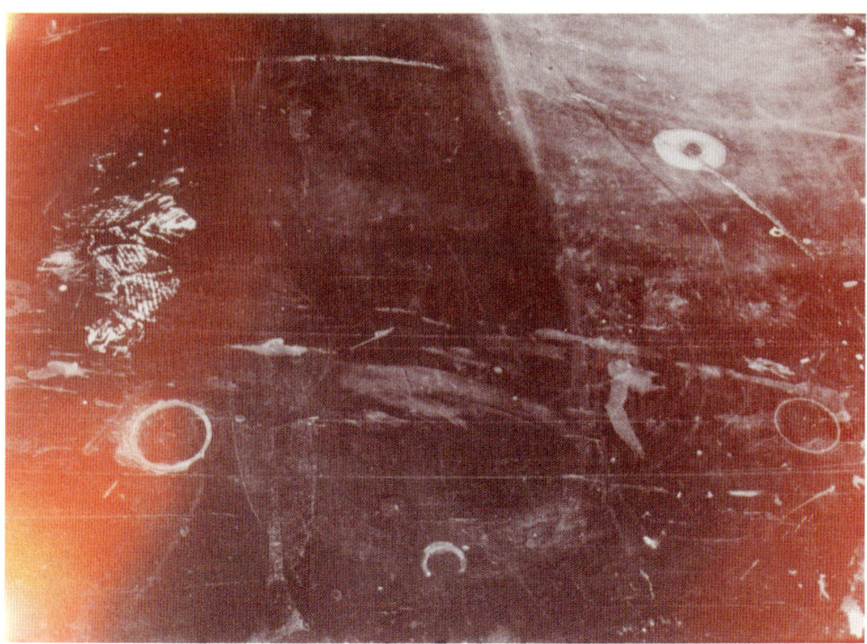

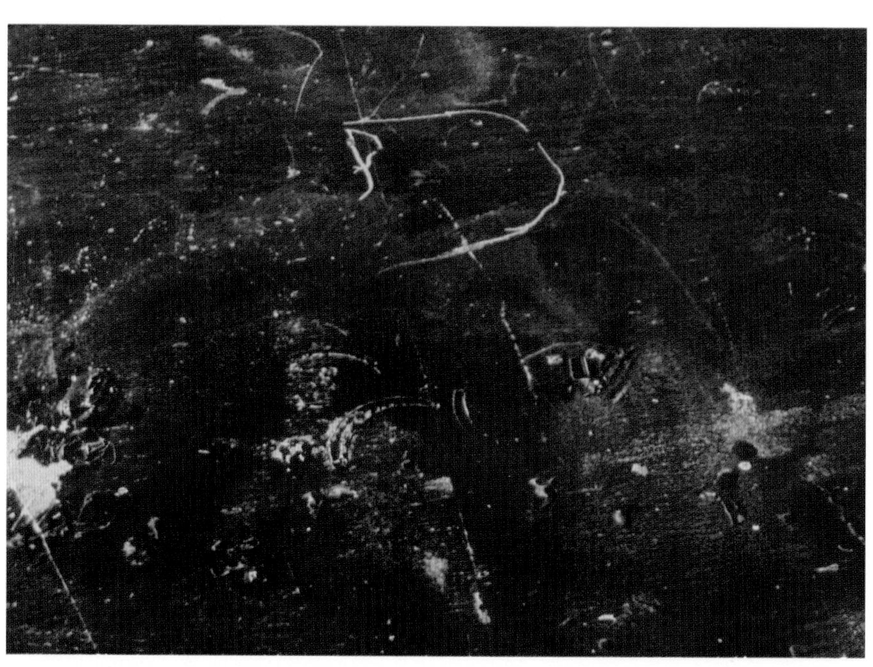

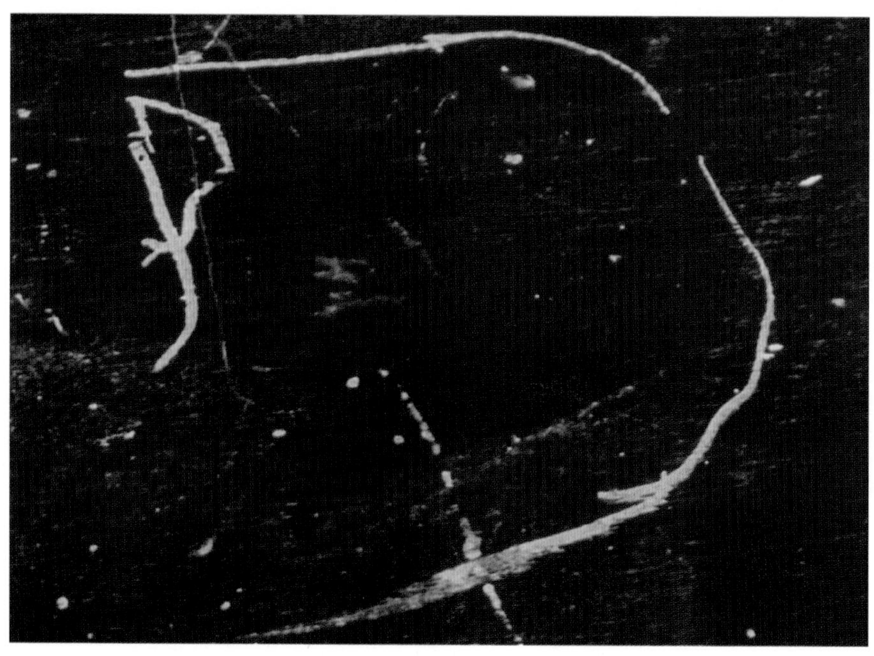

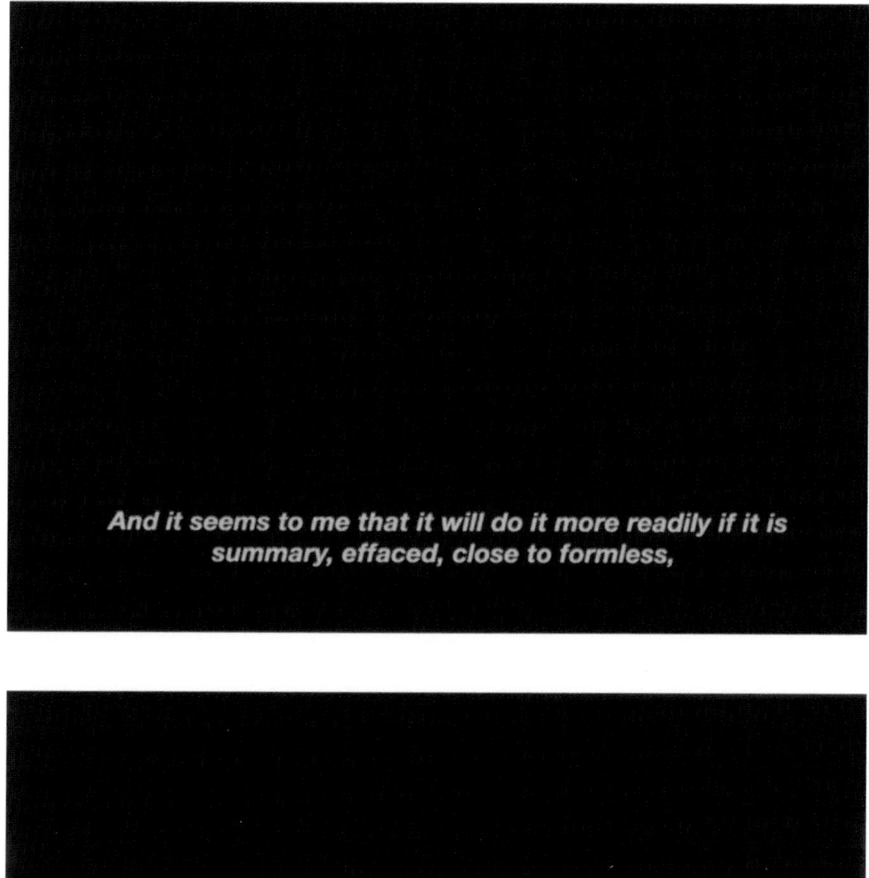
And it seems to me that it will do it more readily if it is
summary, effaced, close to formless,

and if it presents nothing but facts in their purity, and
no formal ideas at all.

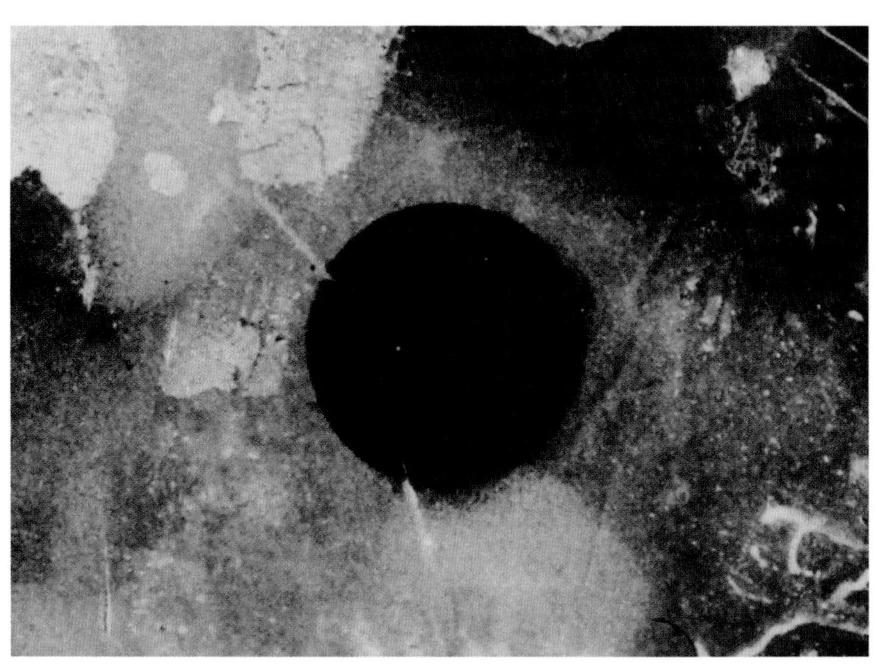

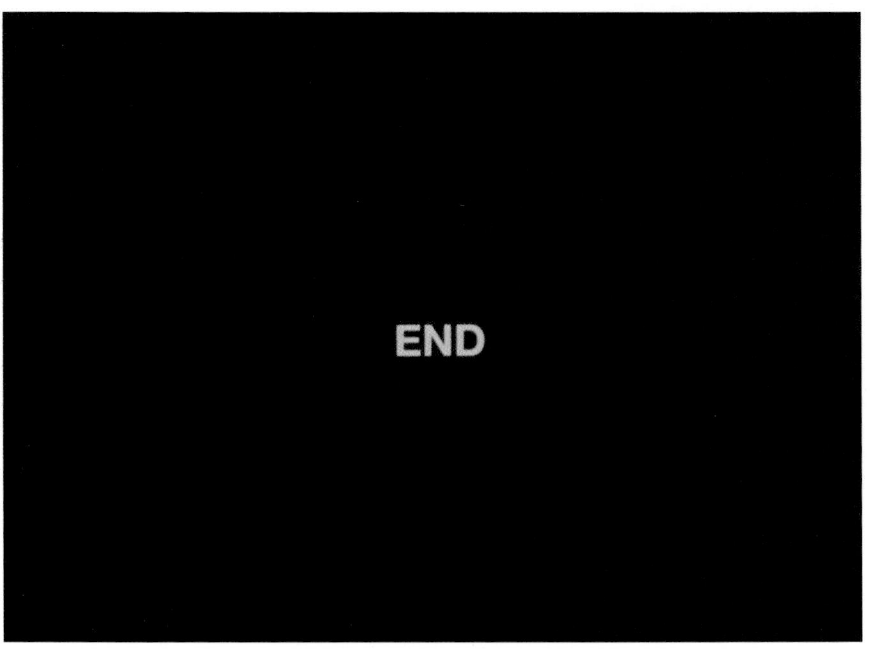
END

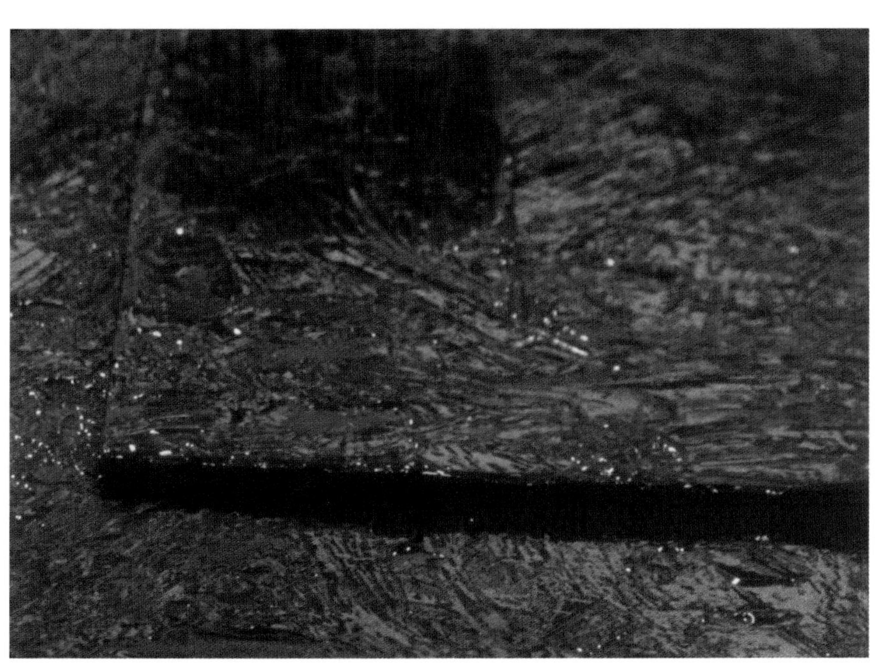

Encre chine, 2012

Encre chine

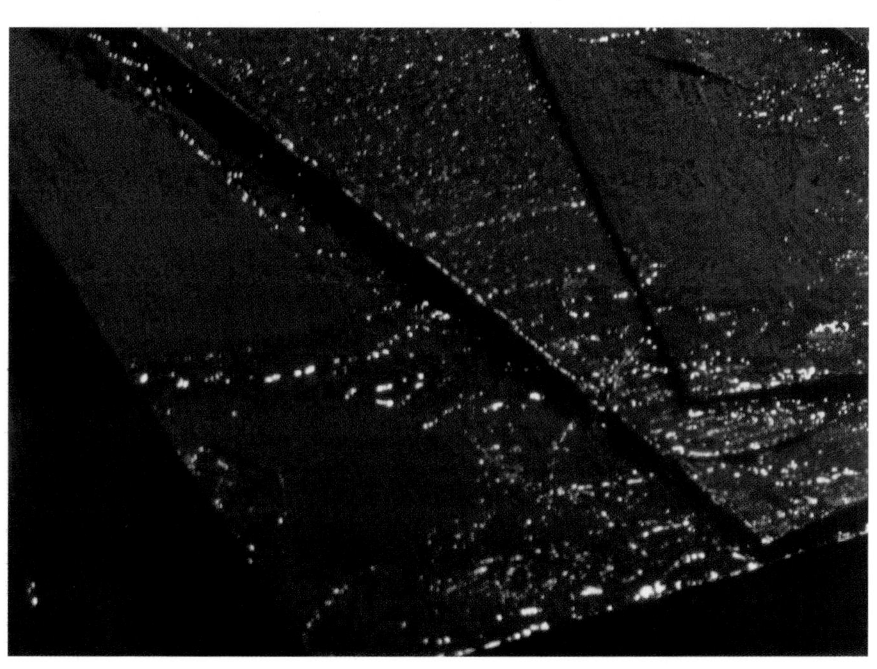

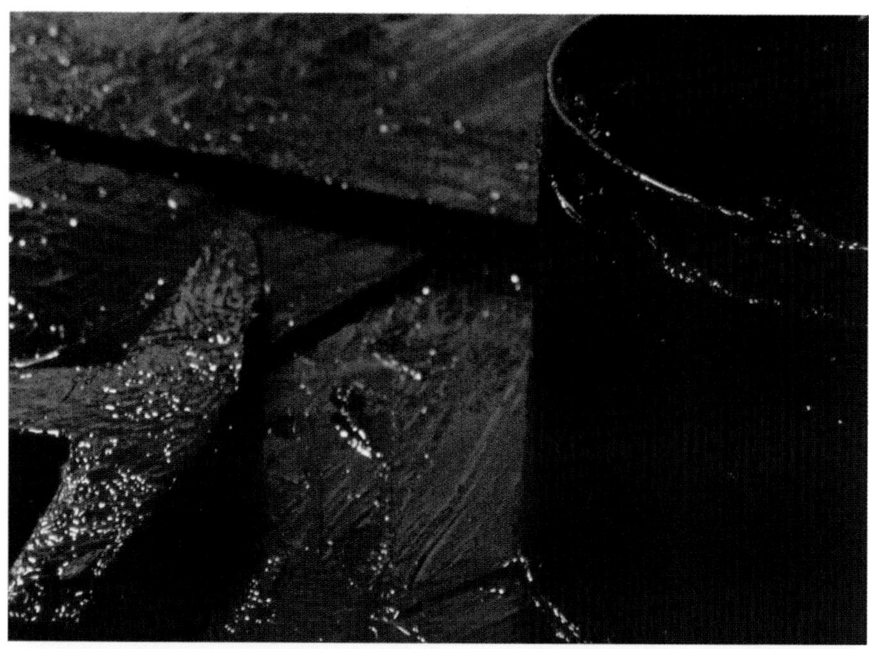

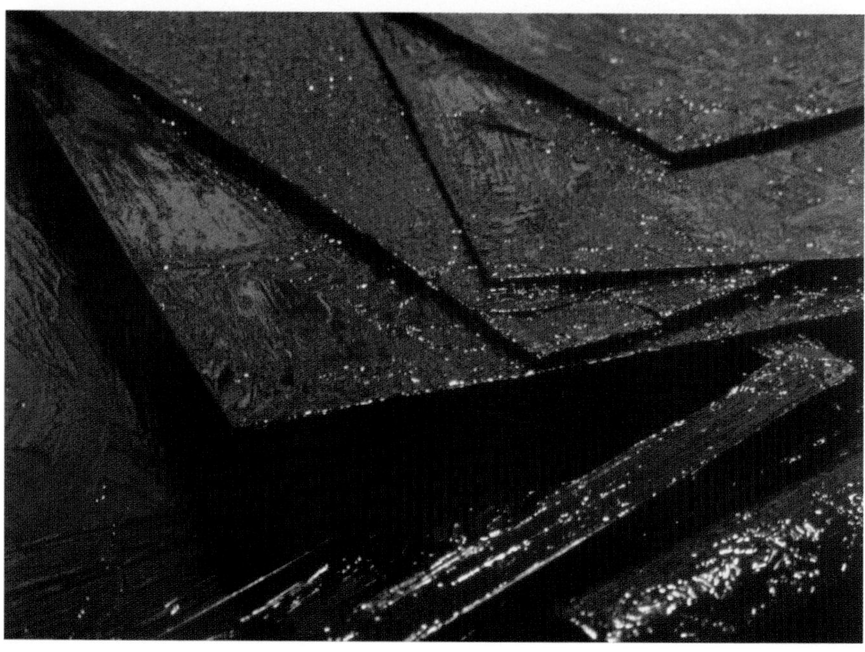

Encre chine

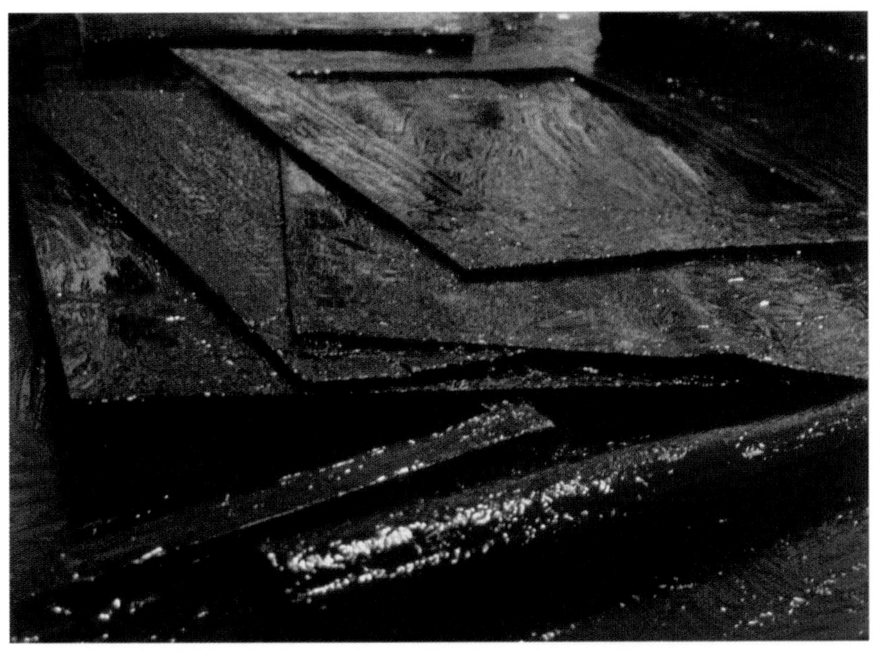

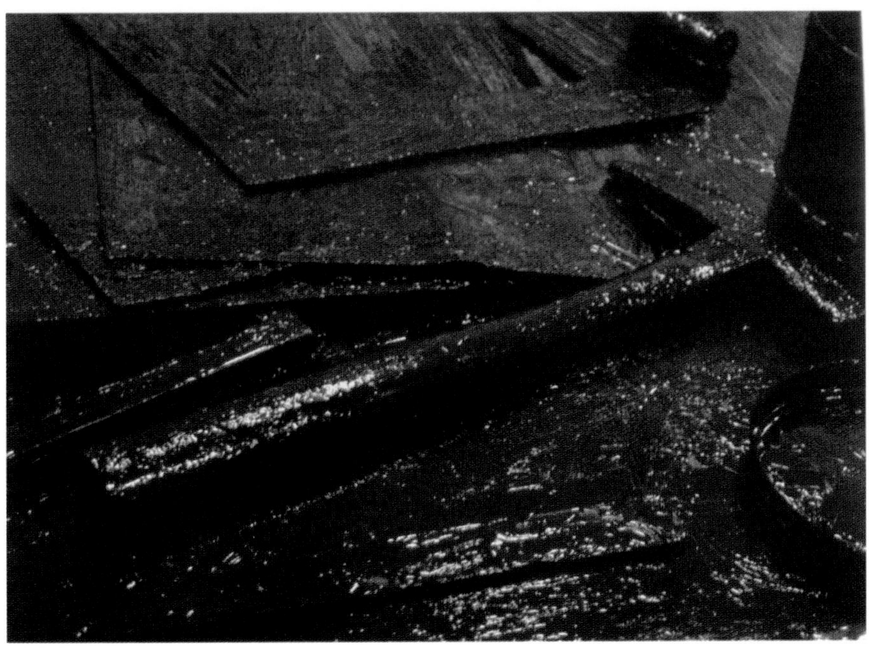

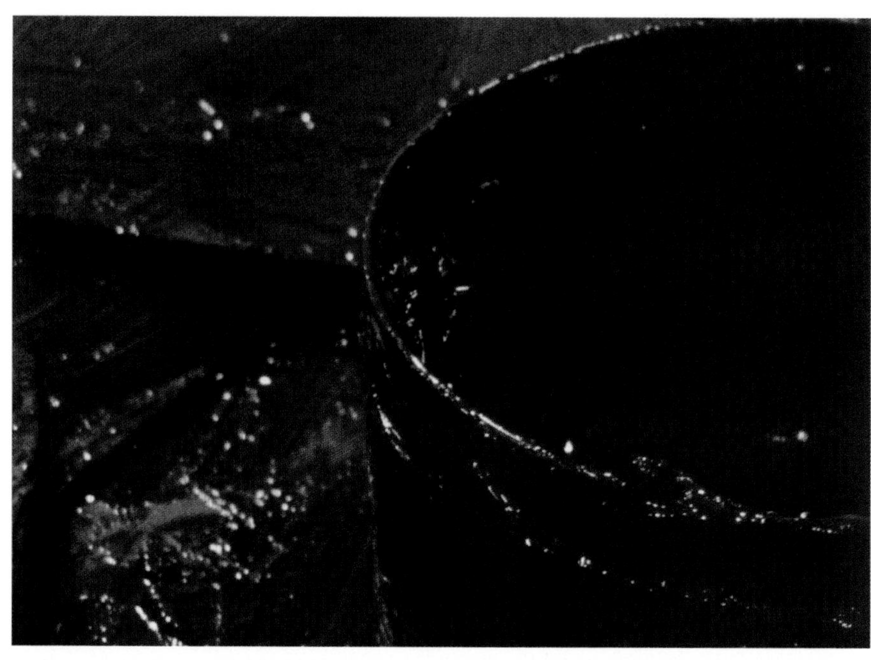

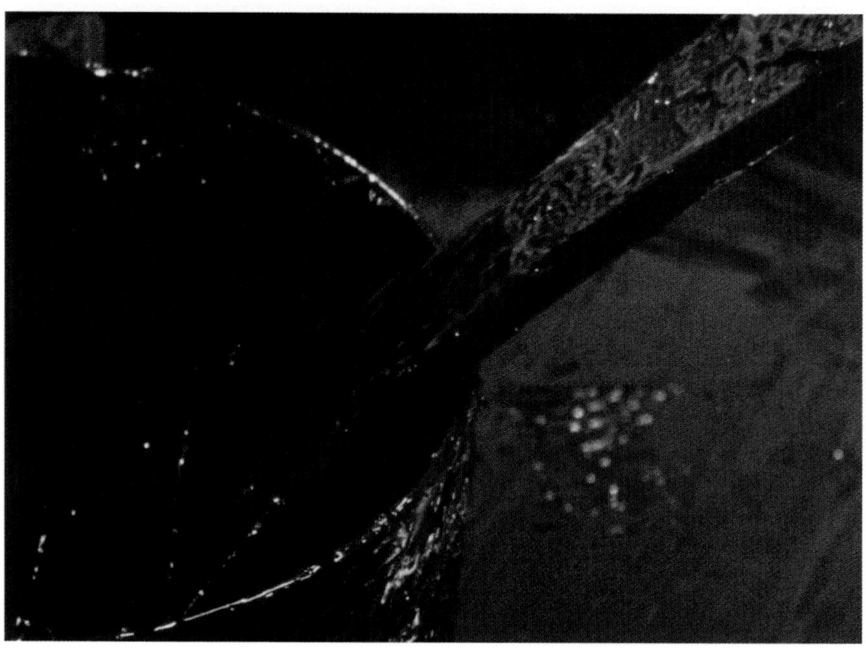

Encre chine

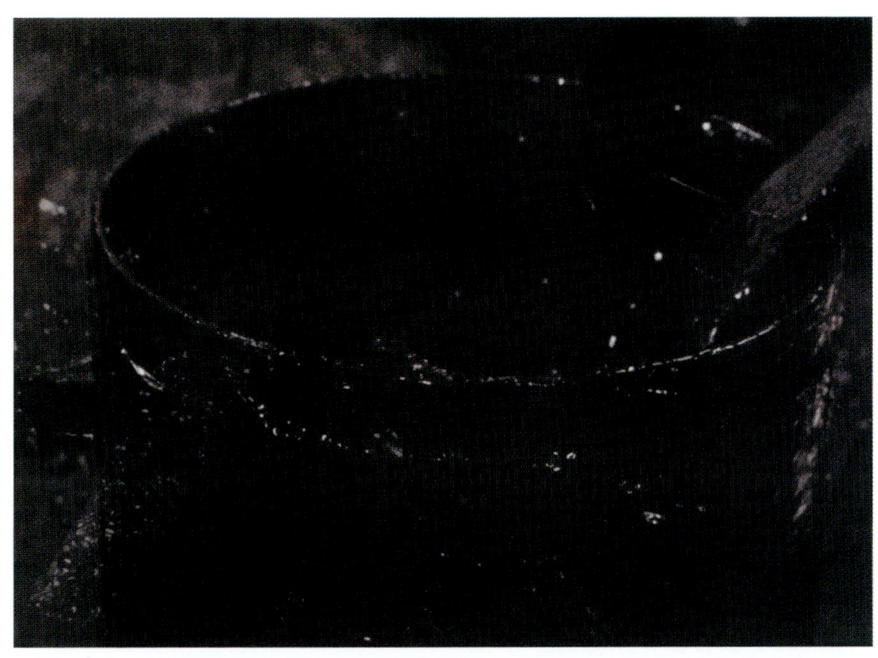

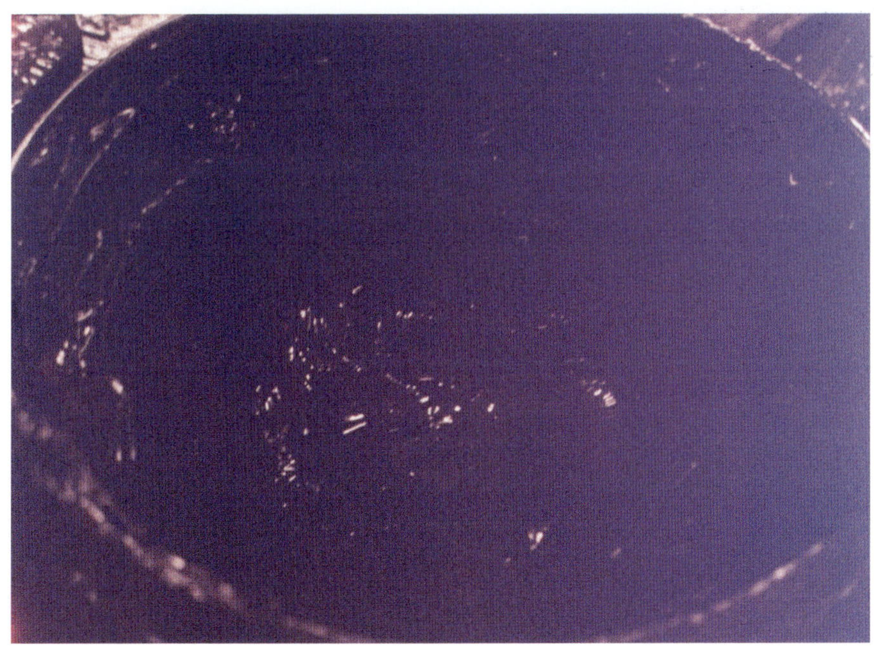

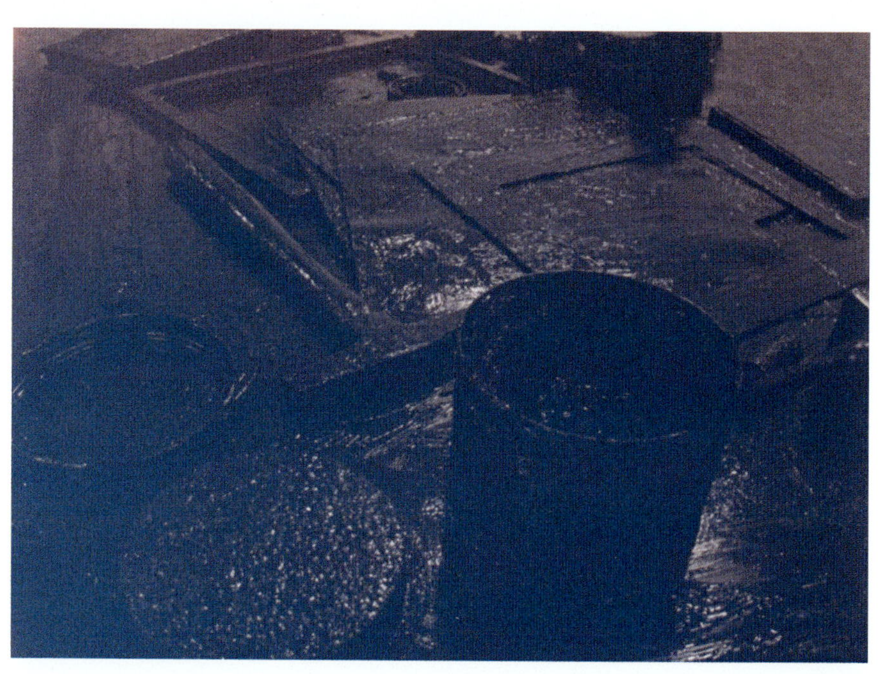

Encre chine

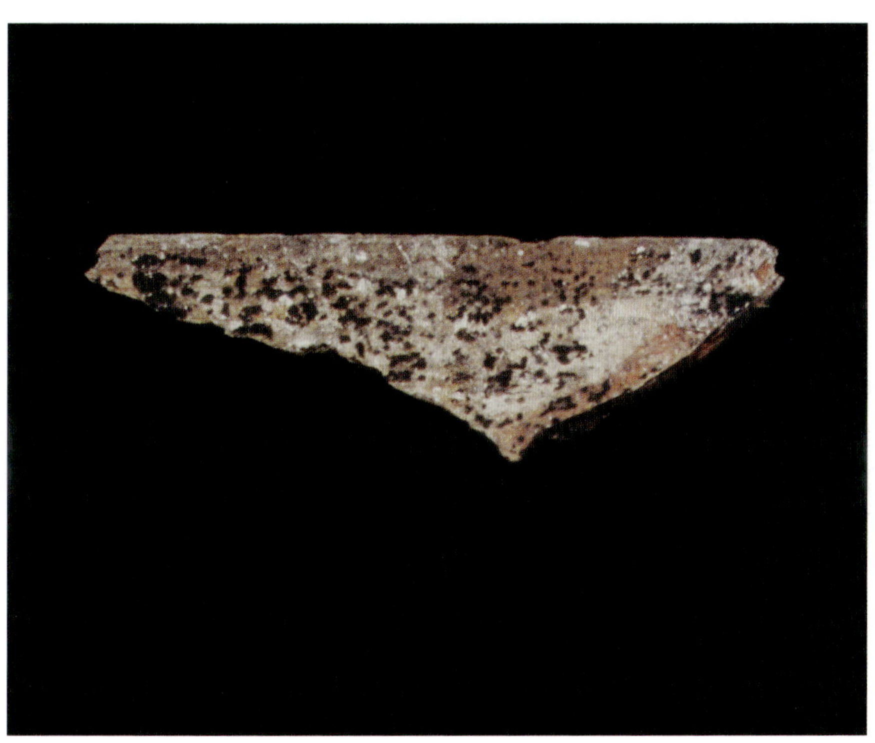

Telegraph, 2012

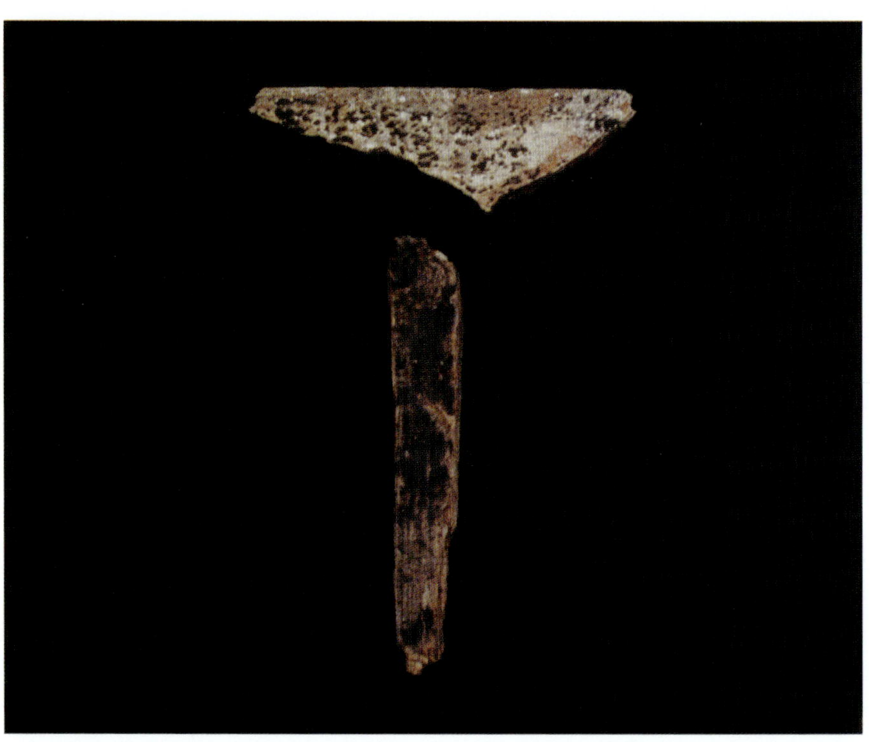

Telegraph

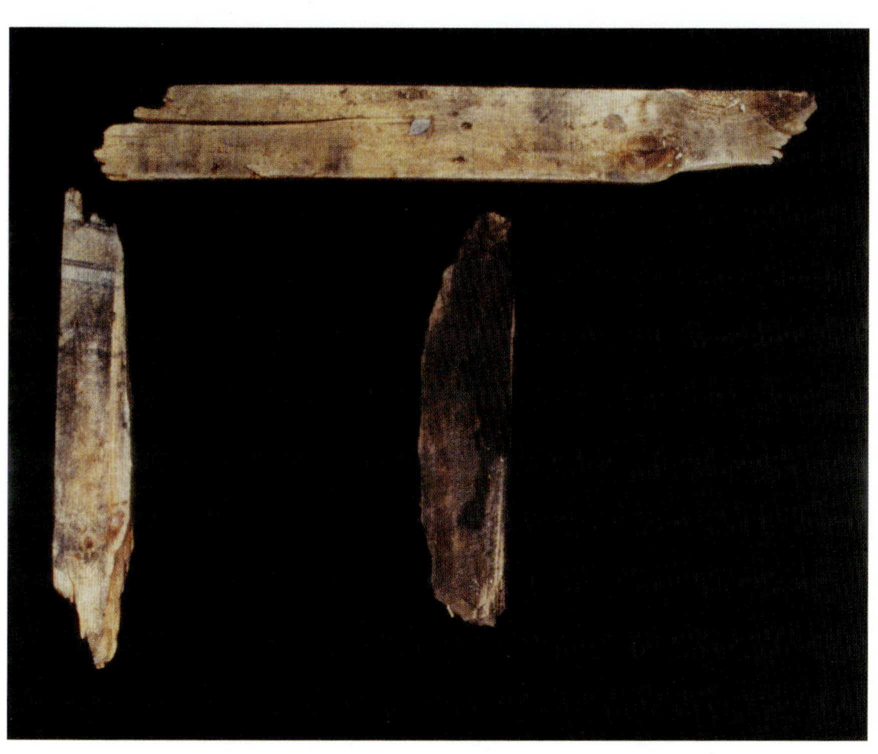

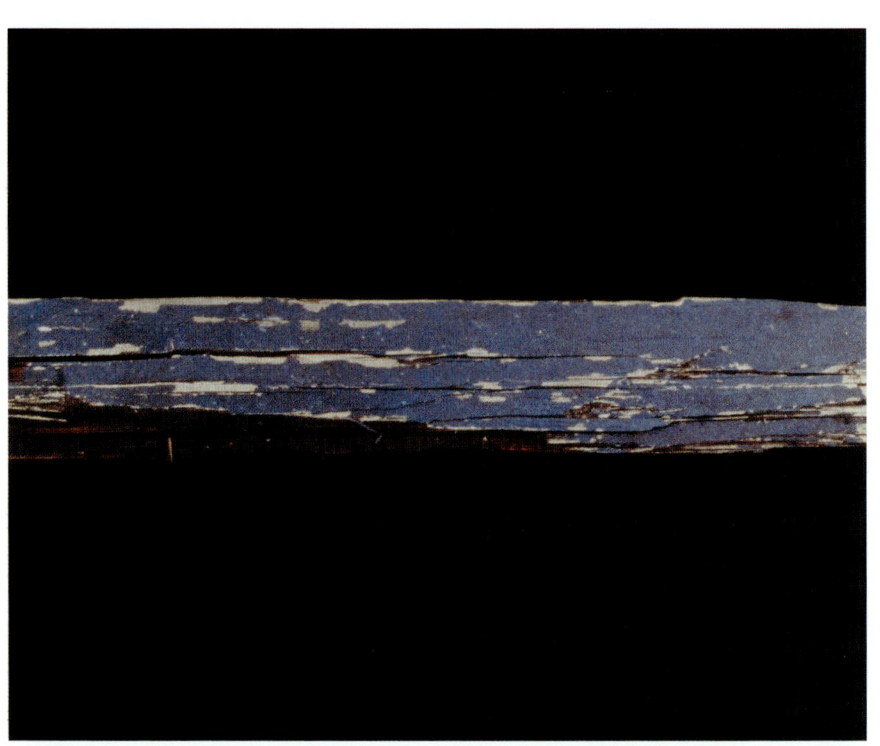

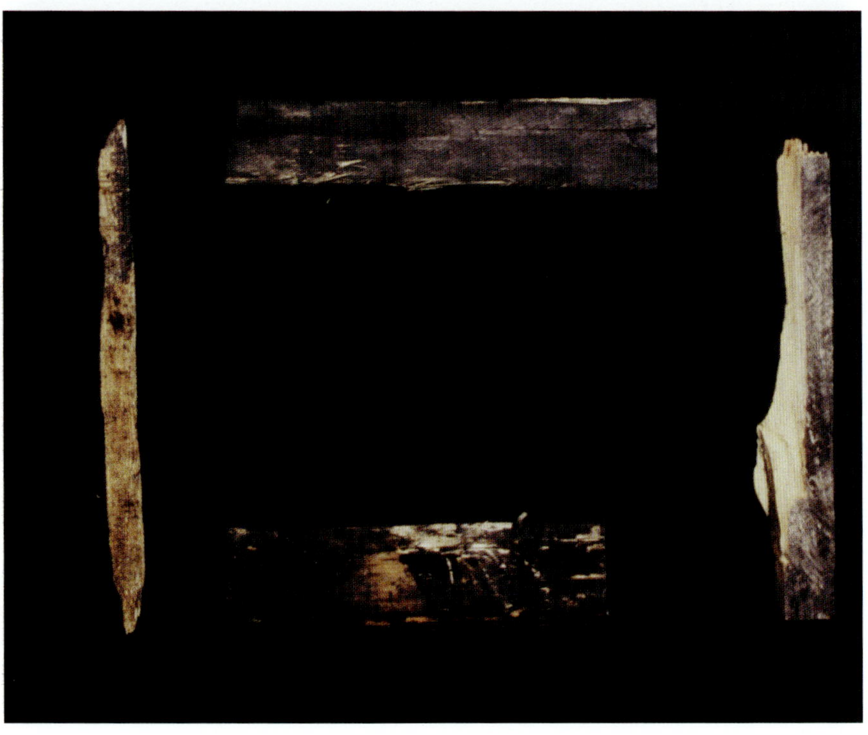

Telegraph

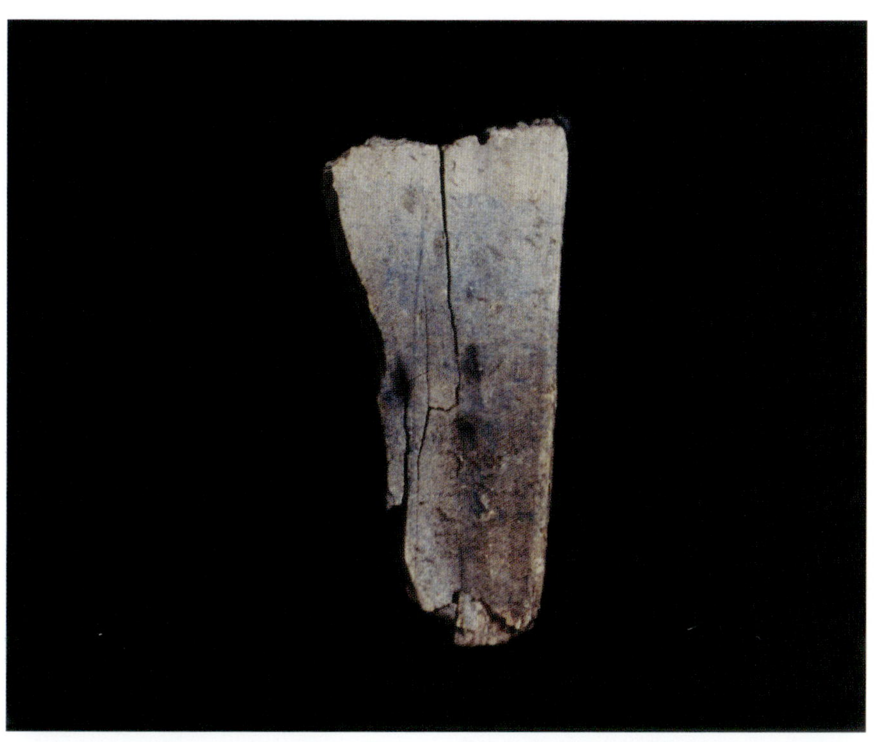

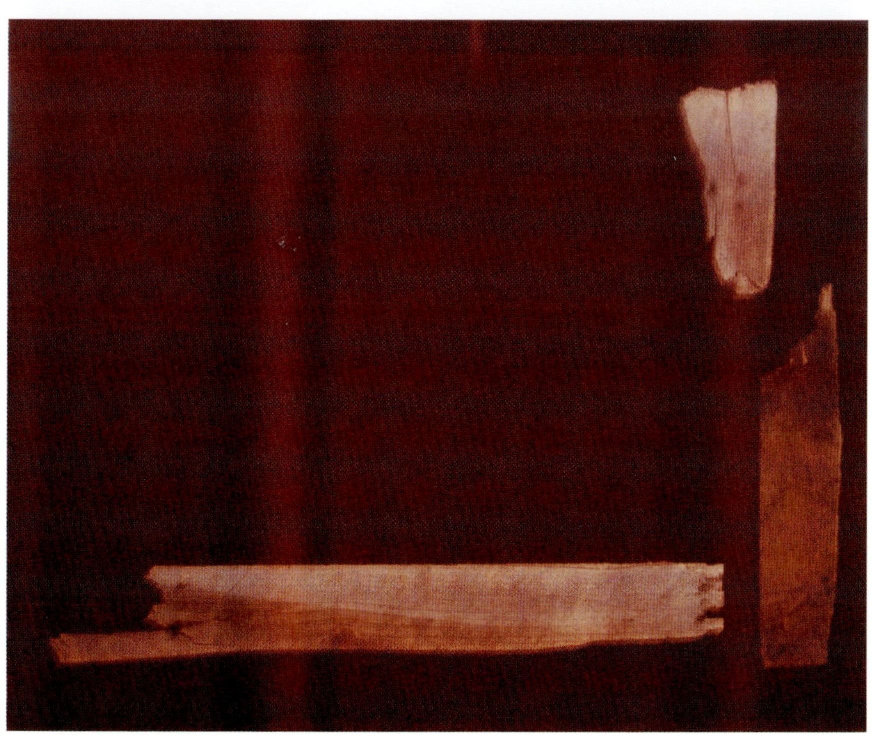

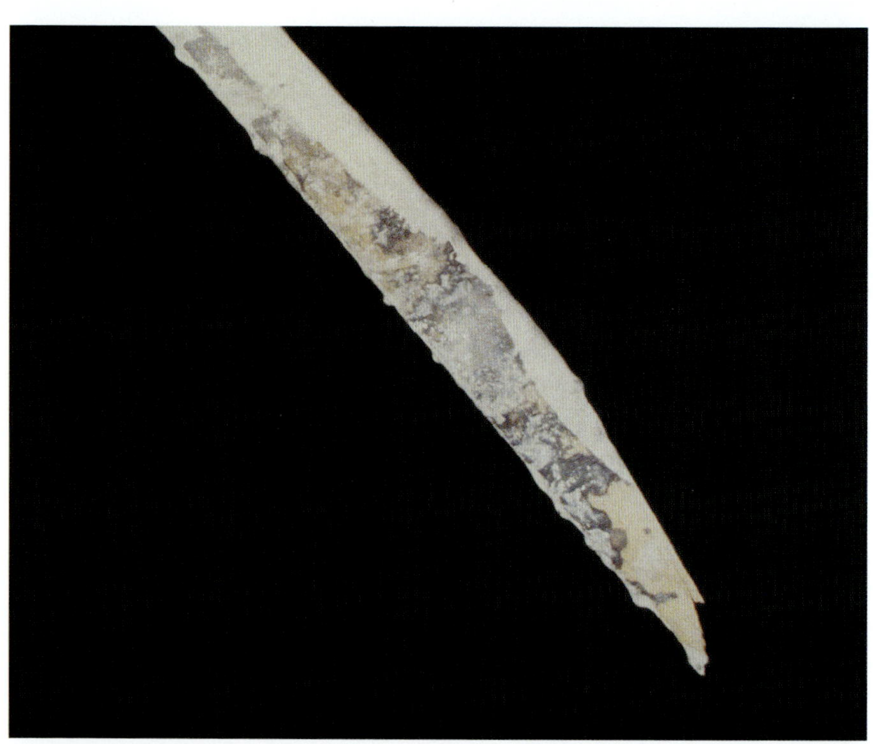

Telegraph

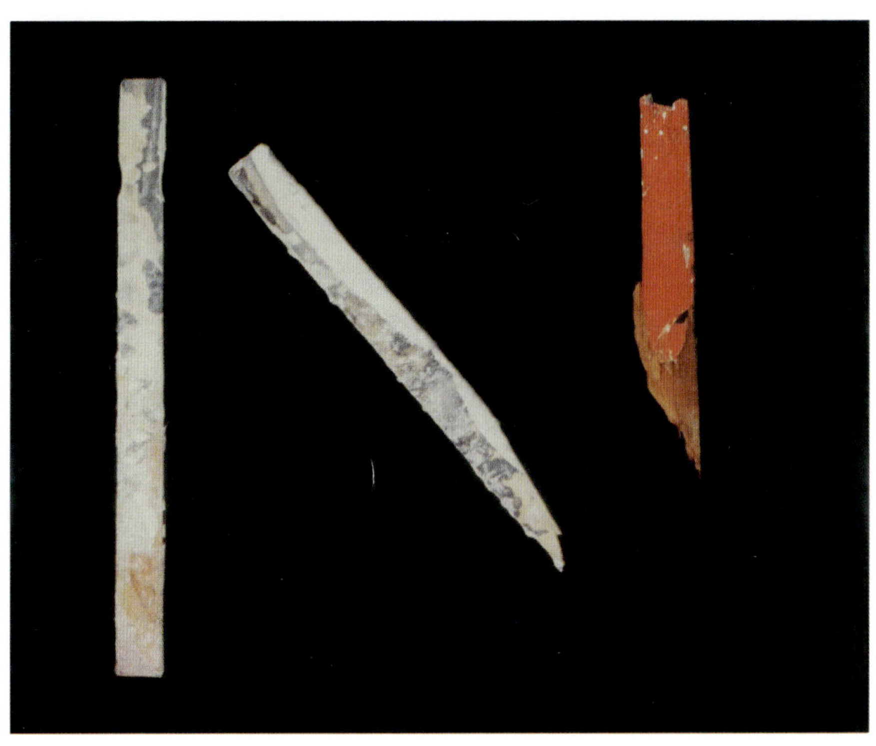

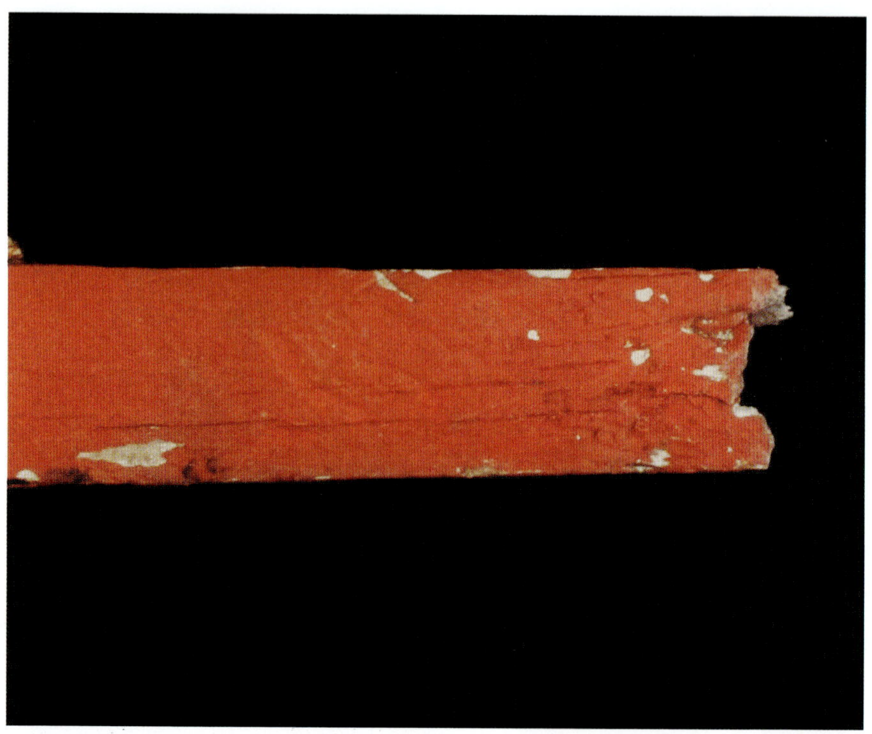

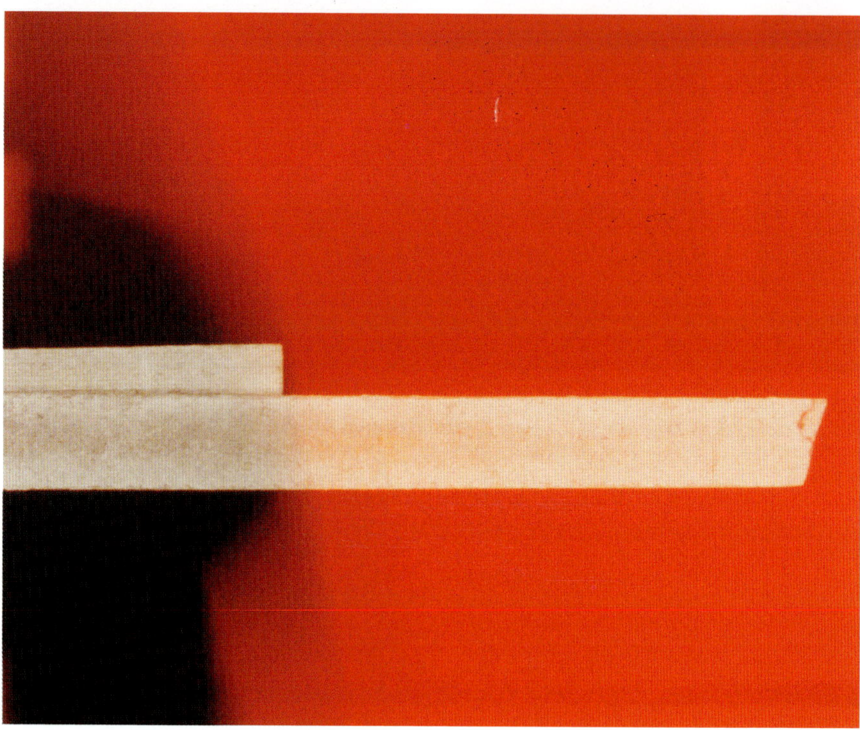

Telegraph

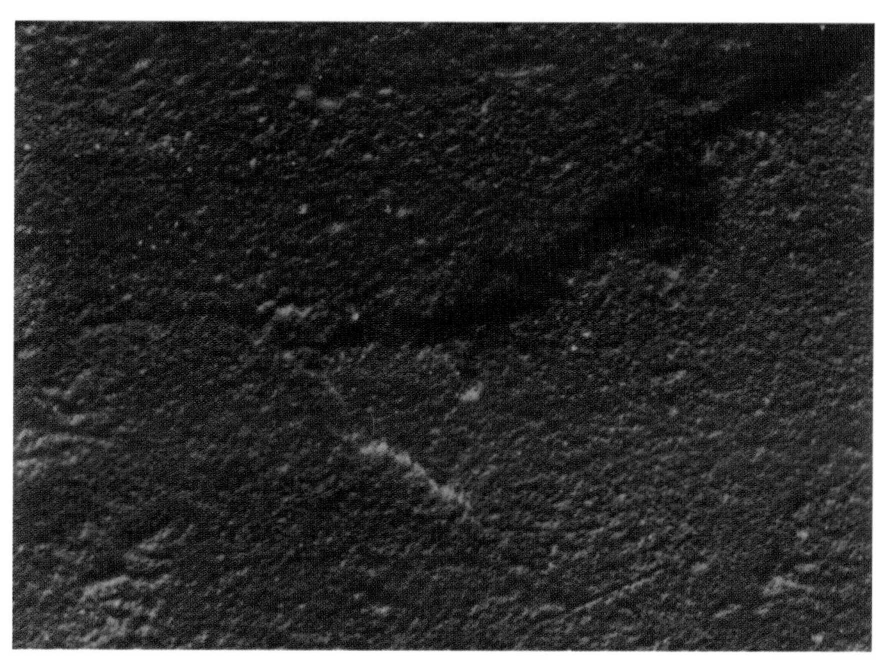

The sentence, 2012

The sentence

95

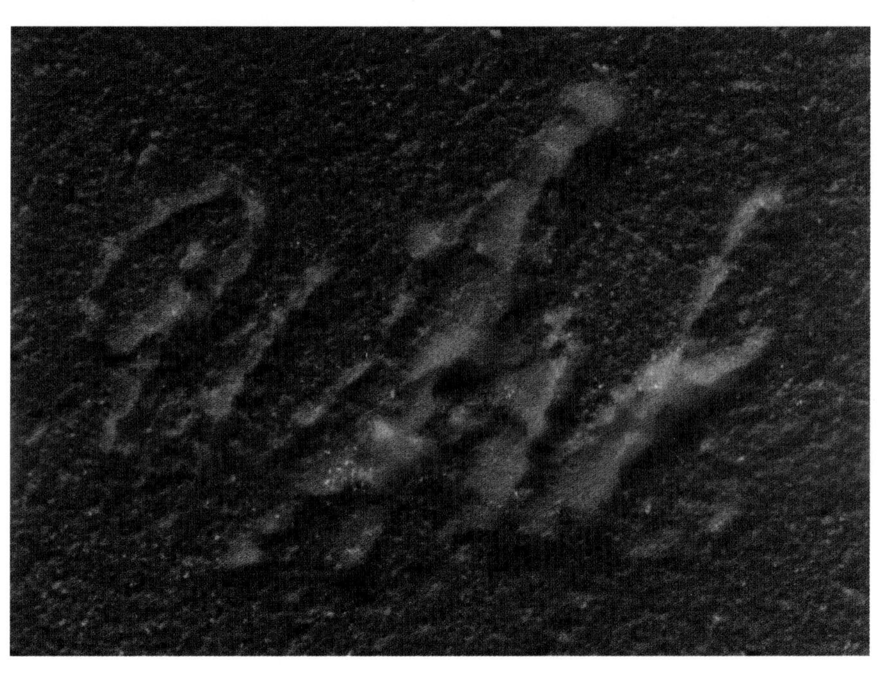

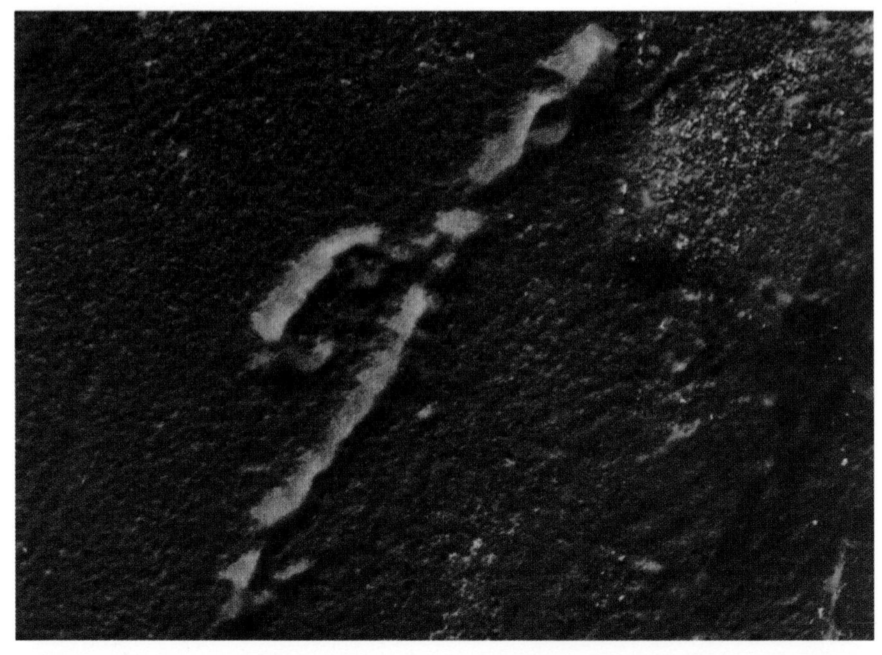

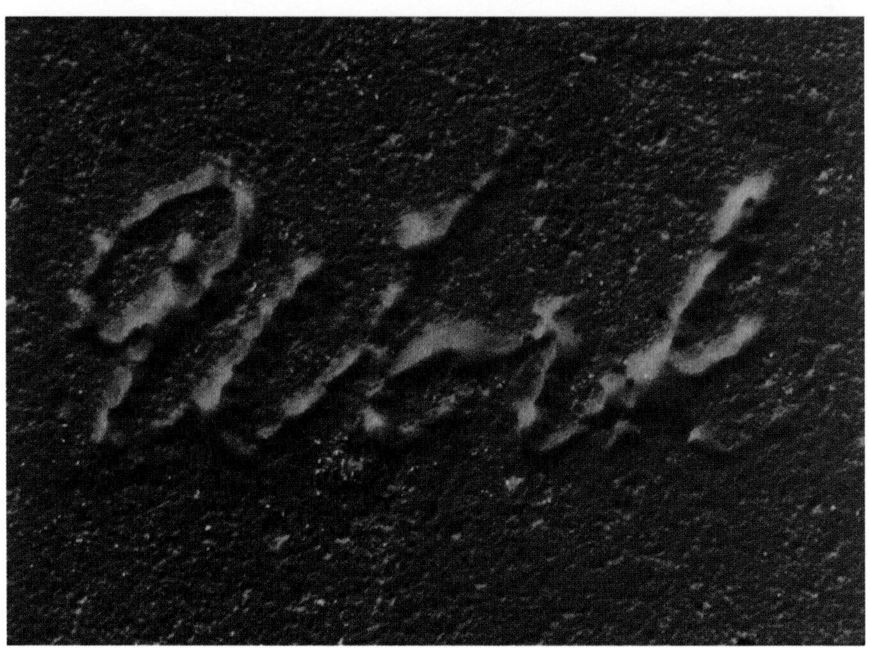

The sentence

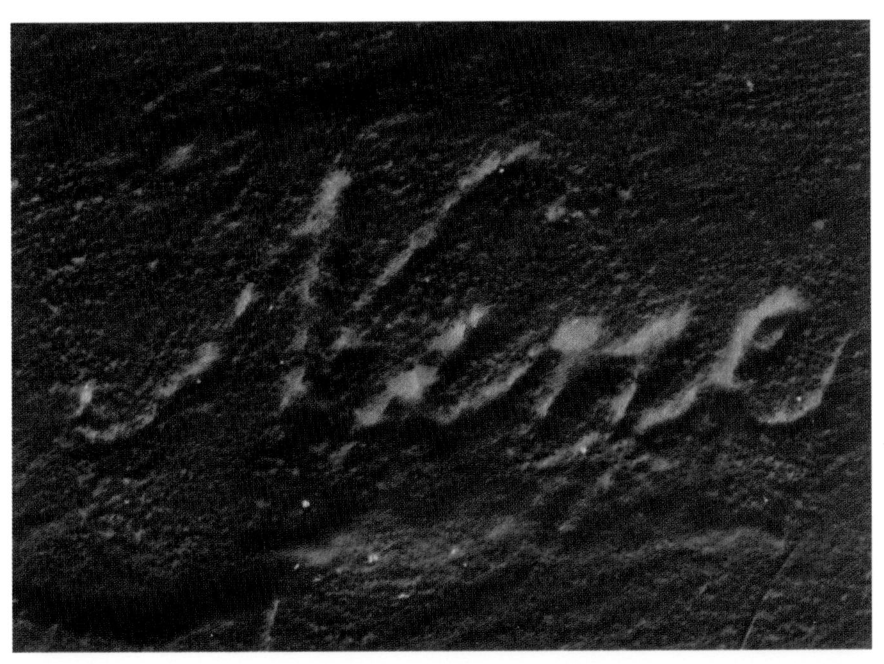

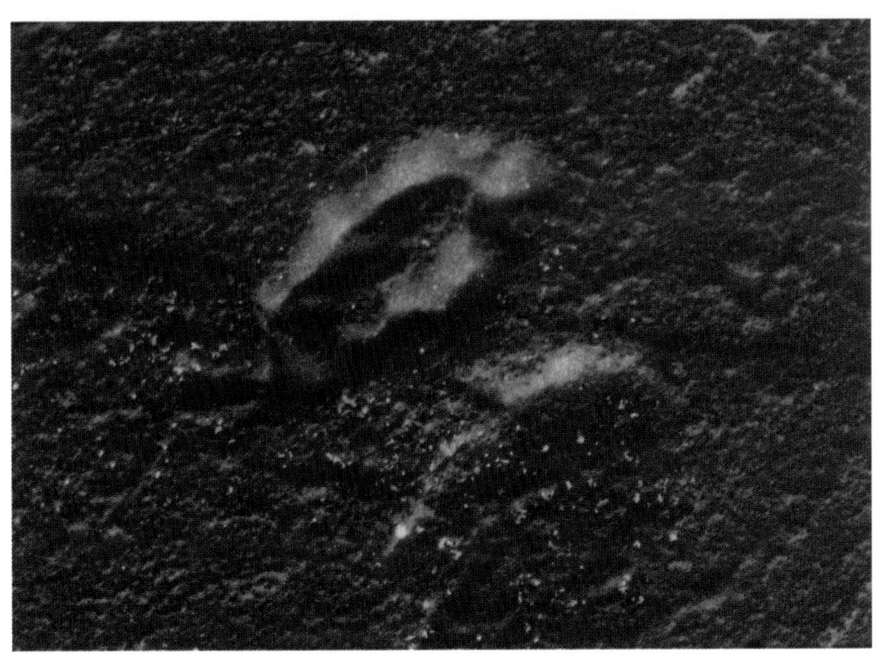

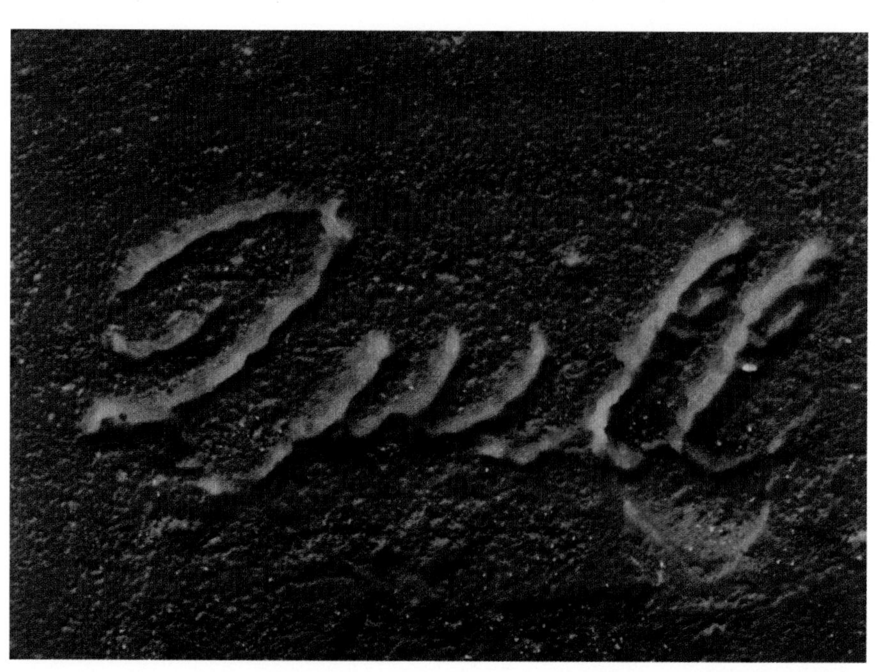

The sentence

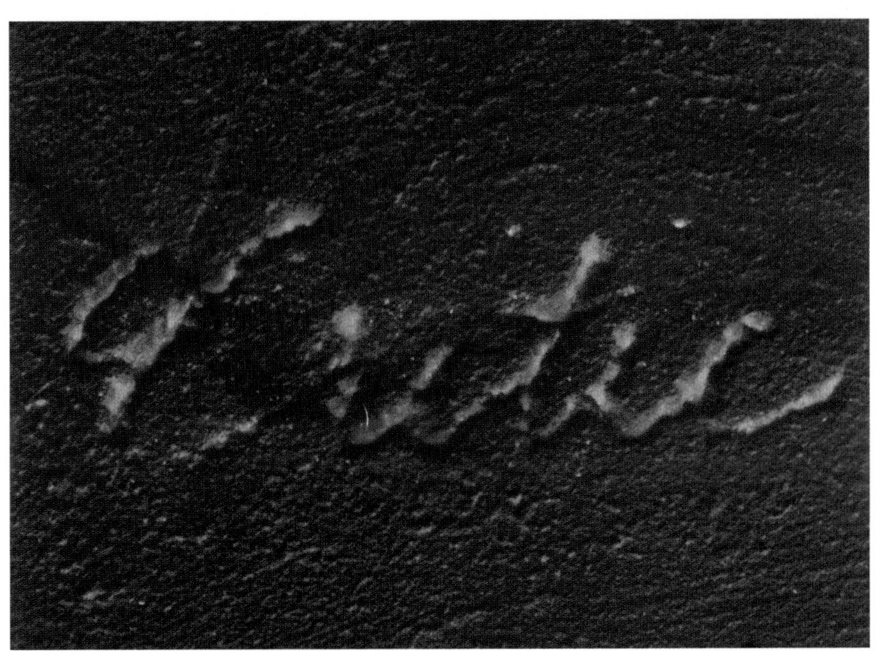

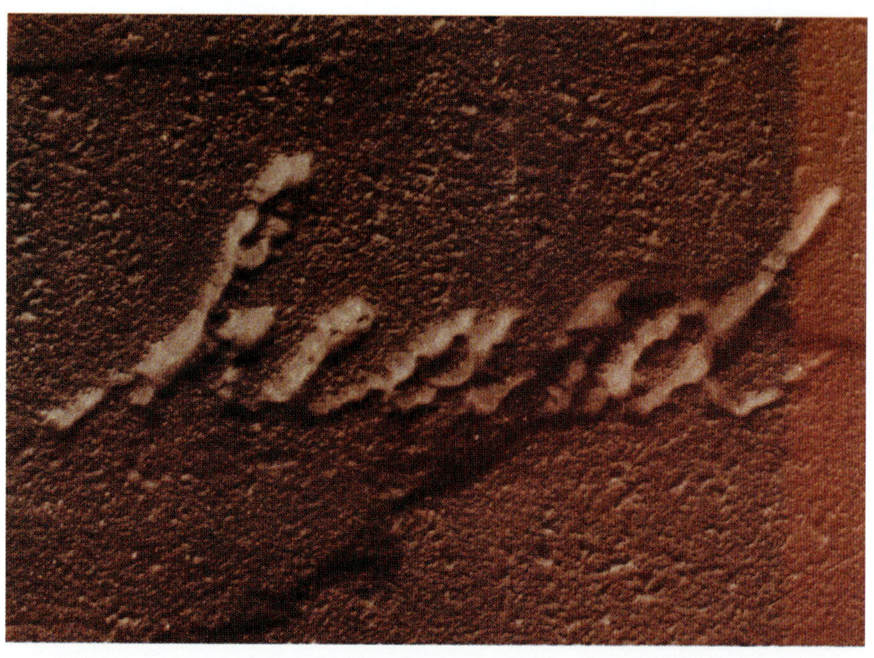

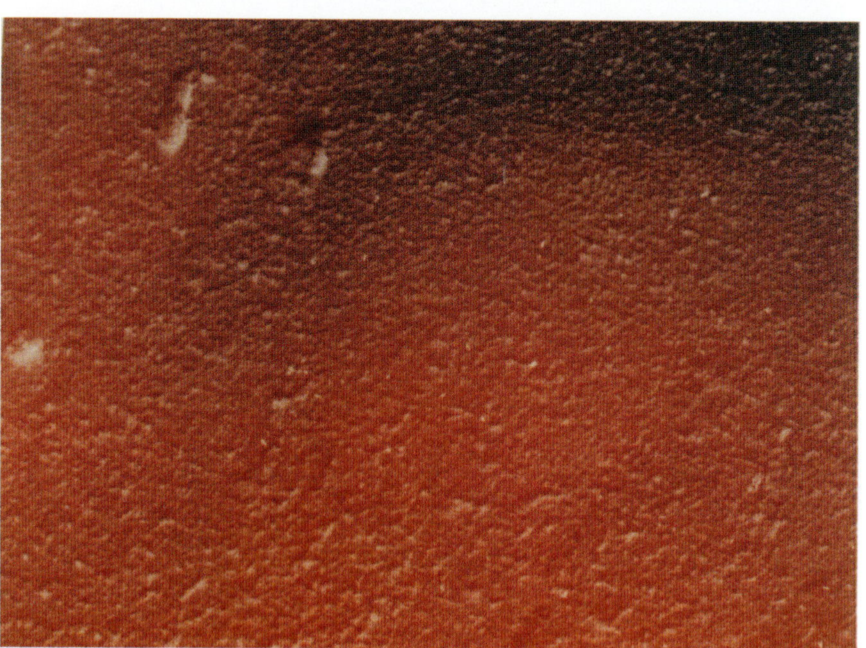

The sentence

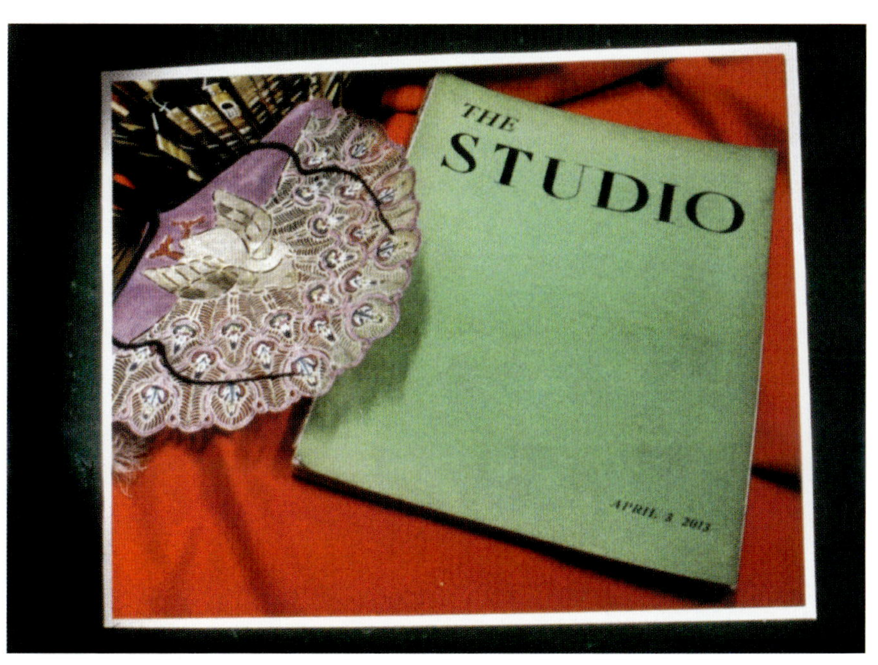

At the hour of tea, 2013

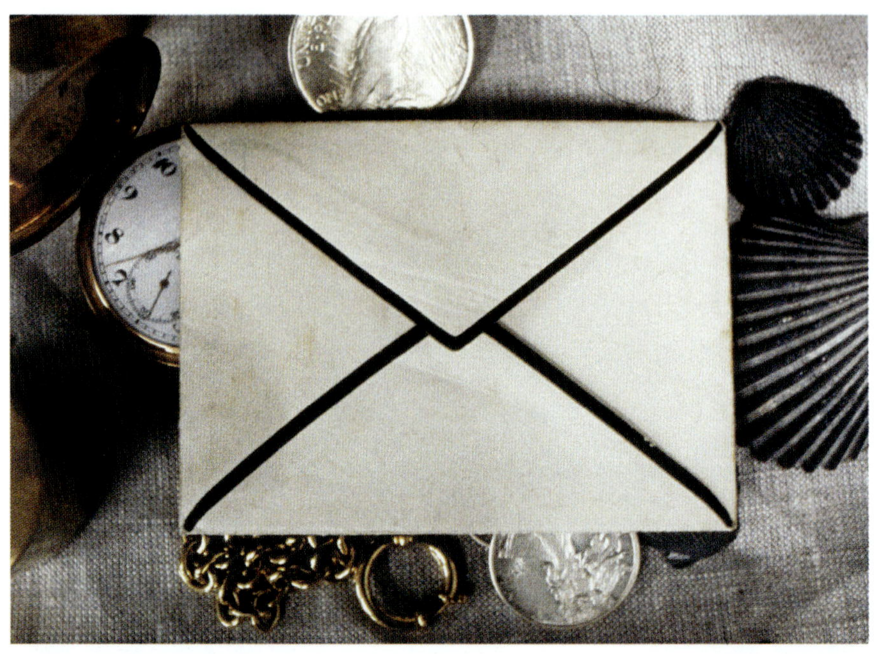

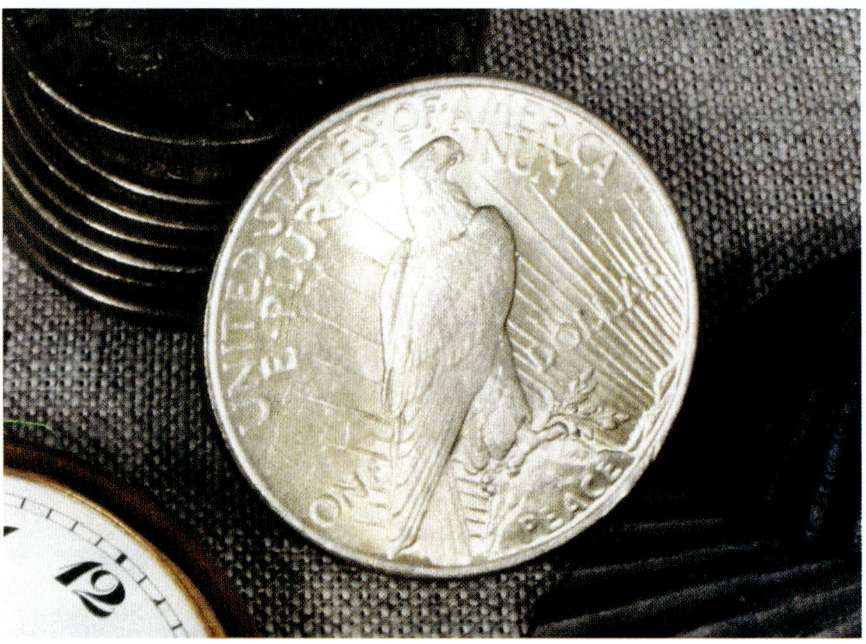

At the hour of tea

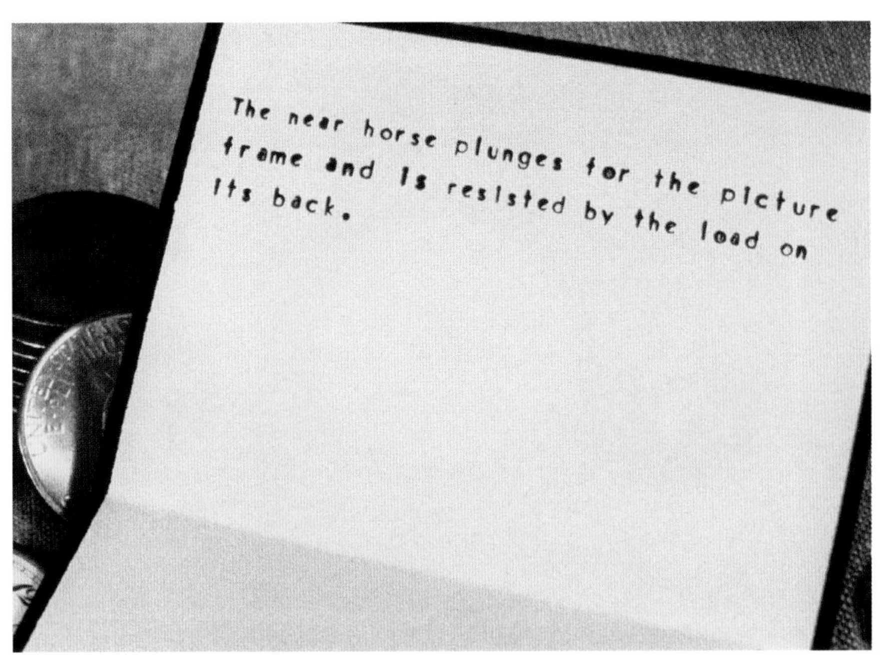

The near horse plunges for the picture
frame and is resisted by the load on
its back.

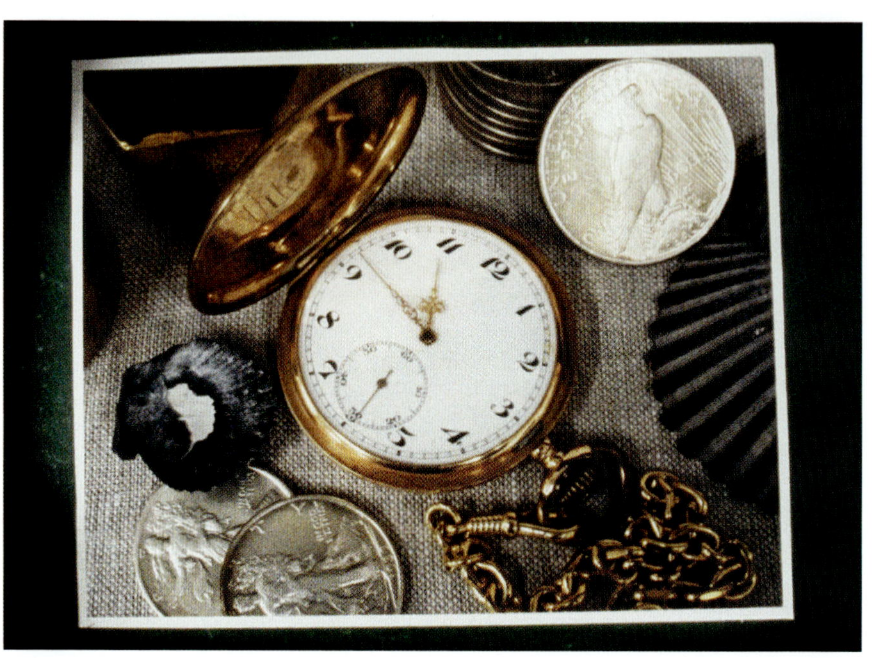

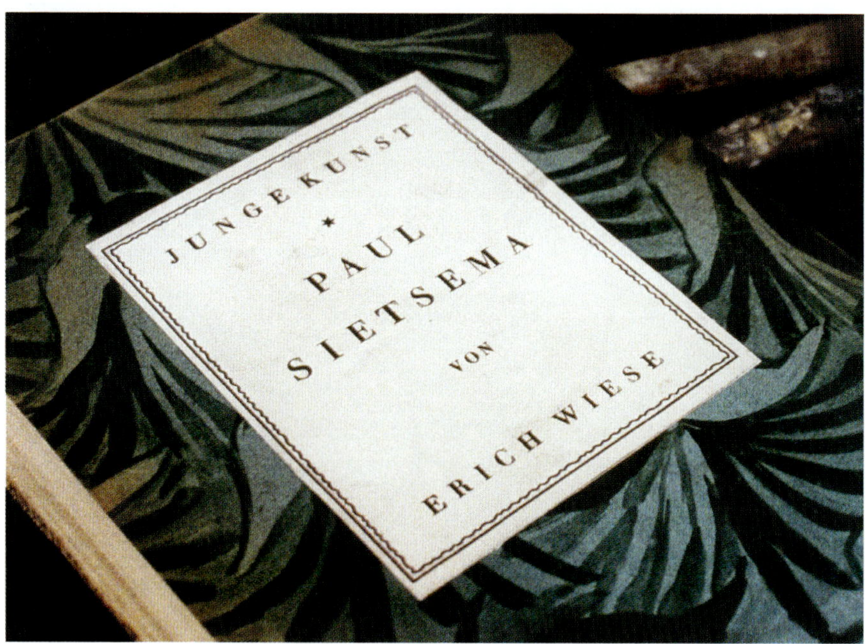

At the hour of tea

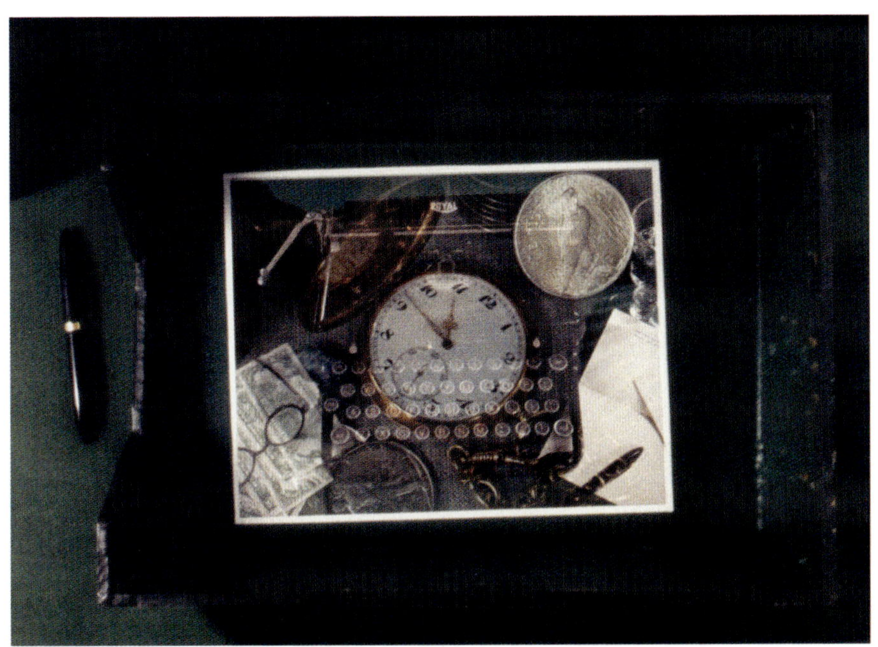

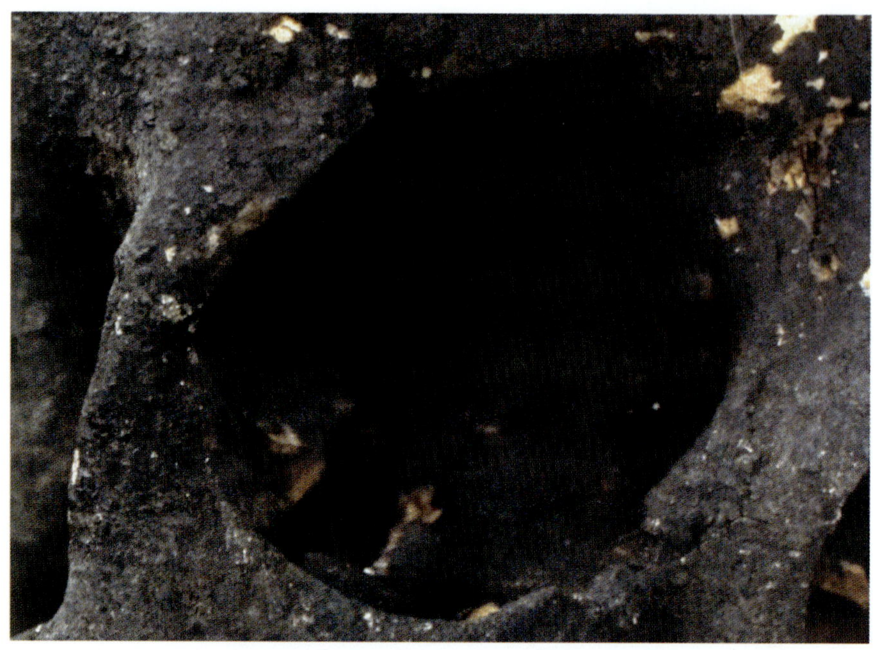

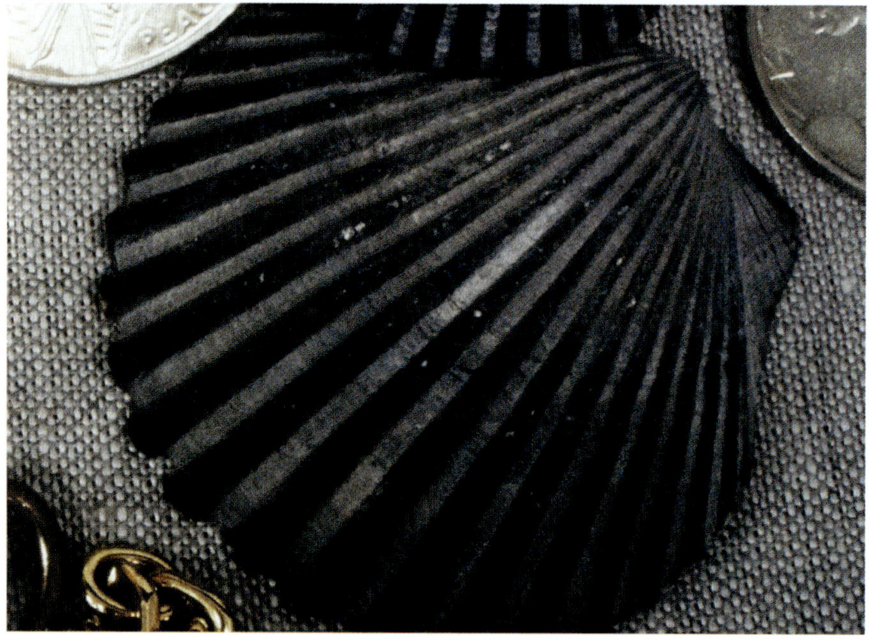

At the hour of tea

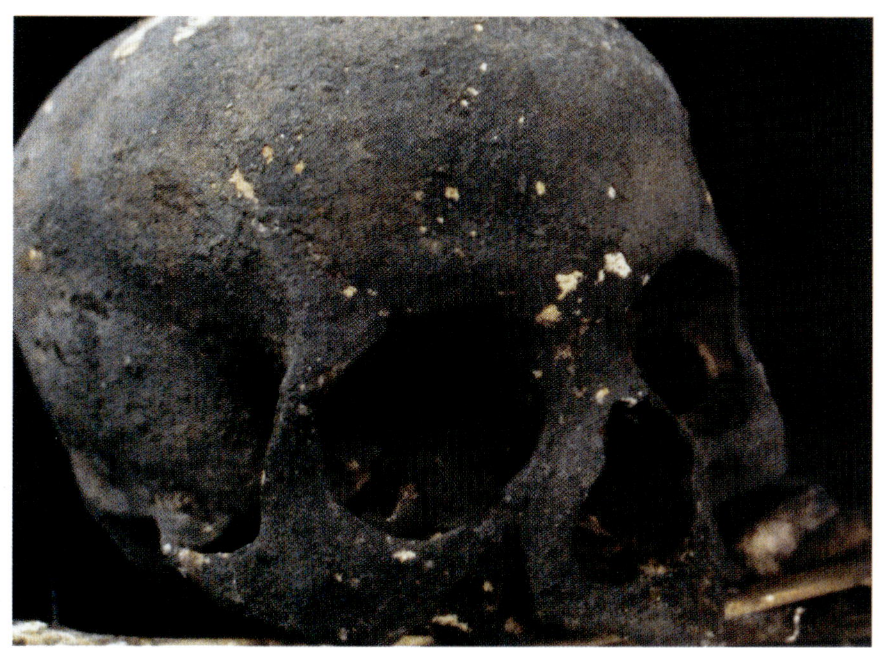

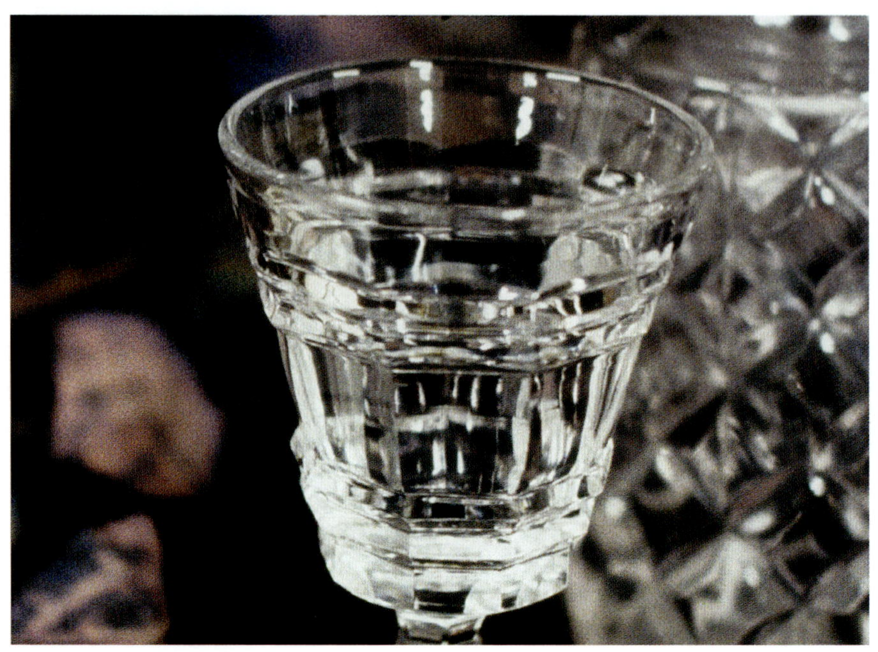

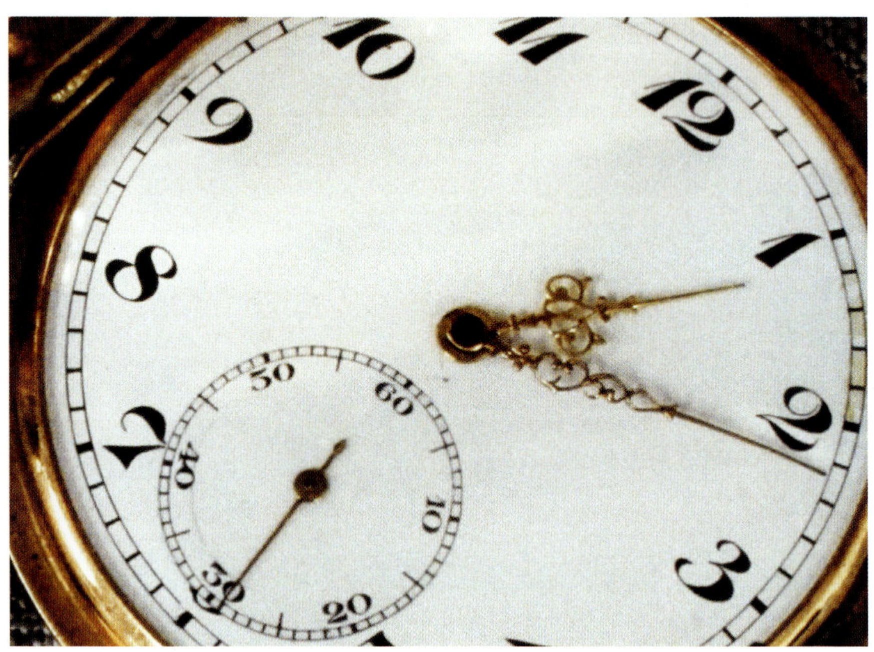

At the hour of tea

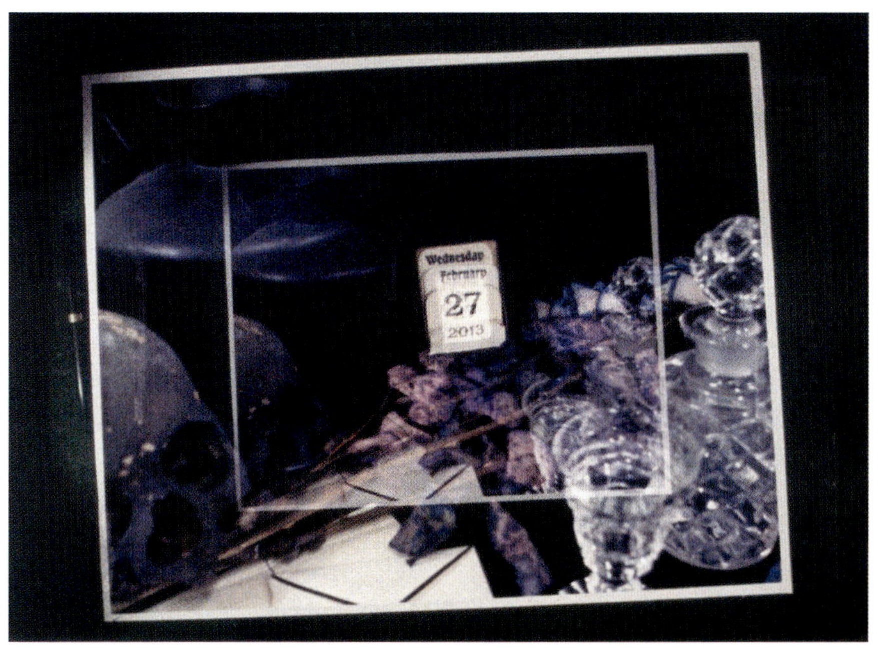

Wednesday
February
27
2013

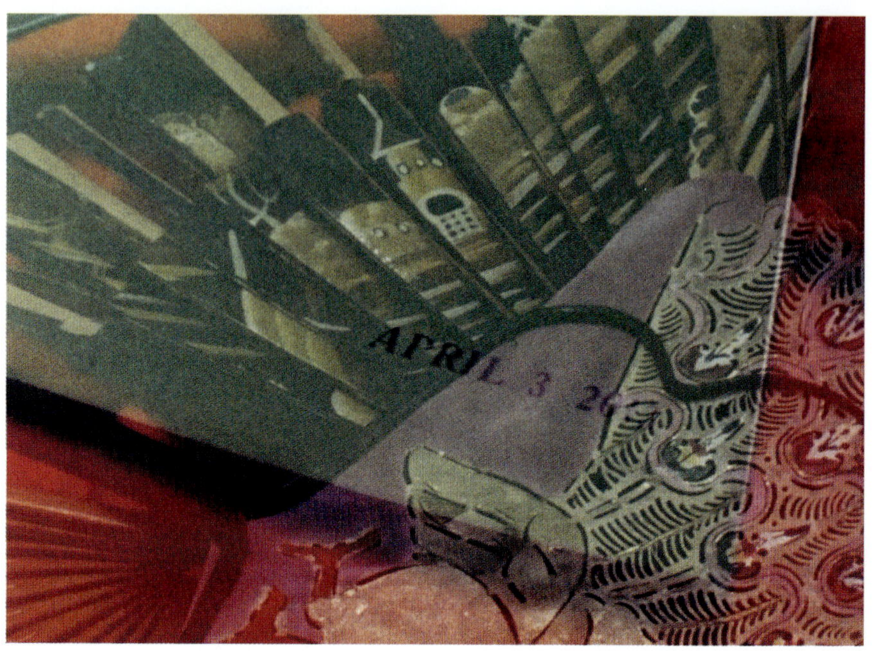

At the hour of tea

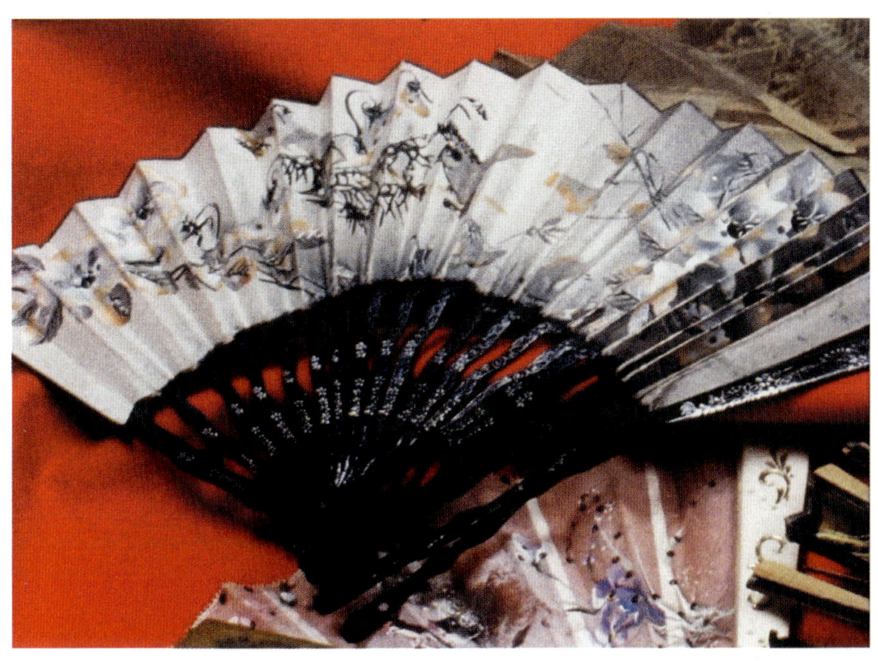

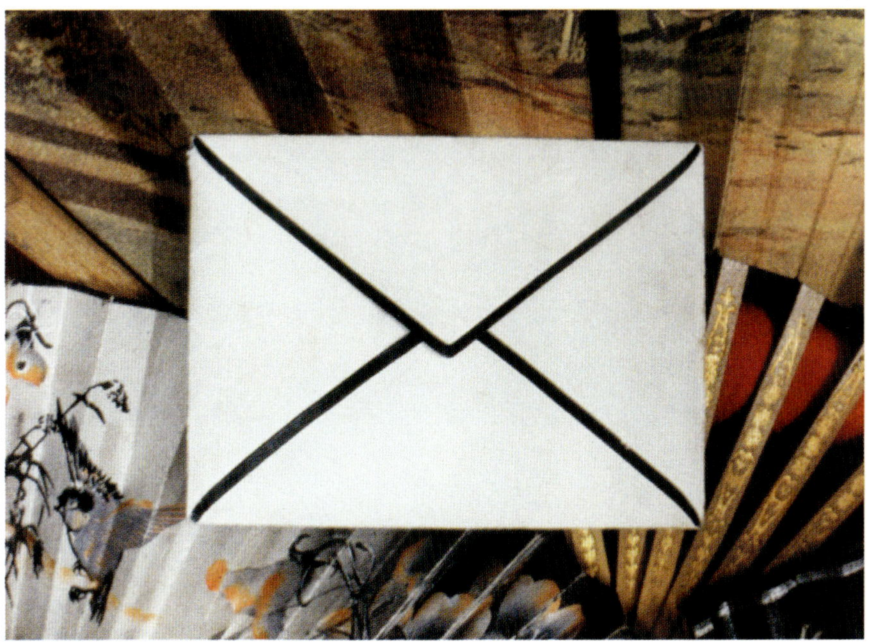

113

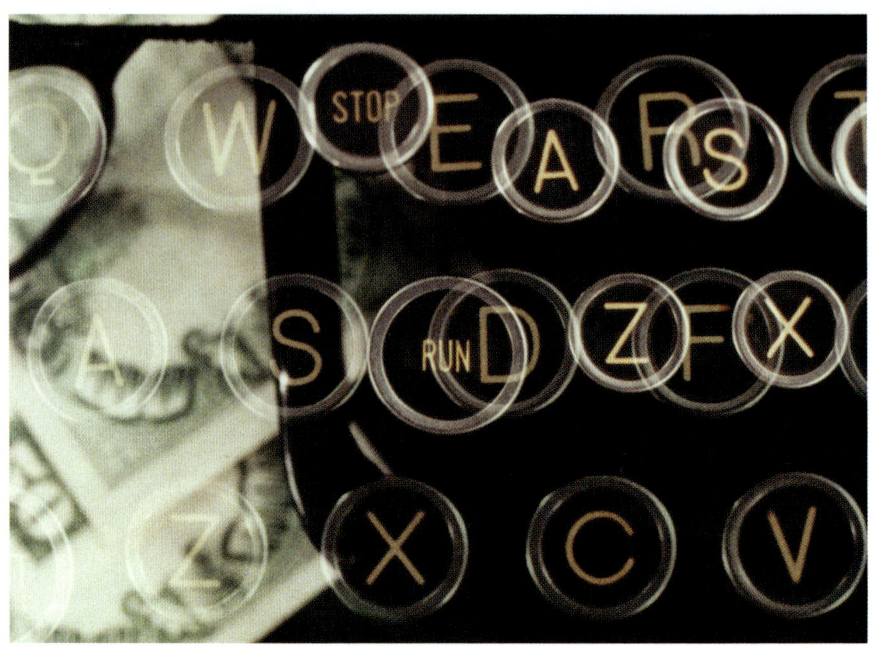

At the hour of tea

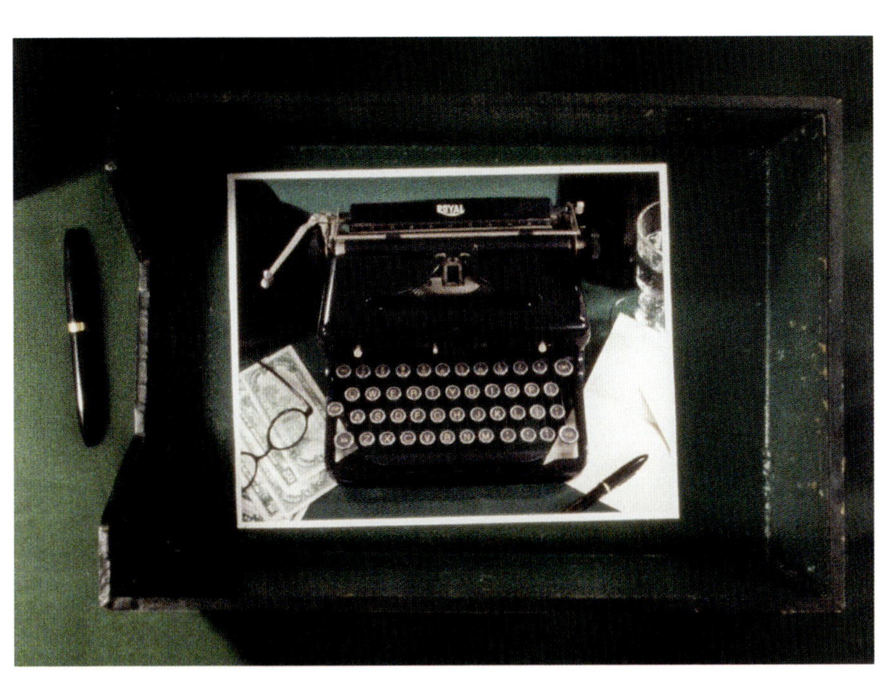

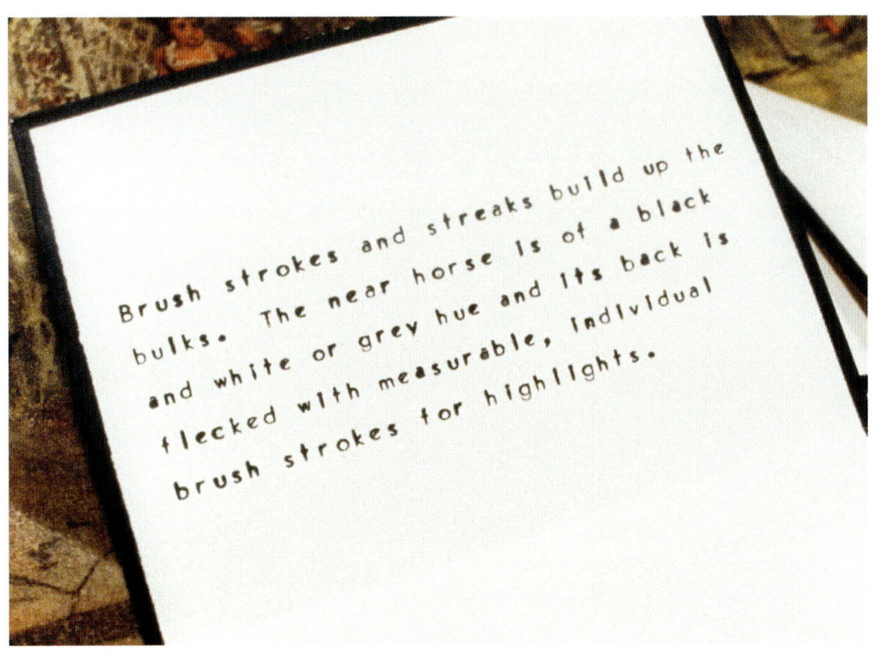
Brush strokes and streaks build up the
bulks. The near horse is of a black
and white or grey hue and its back is
flecked with measurable, individual
brush strokes for highlights.

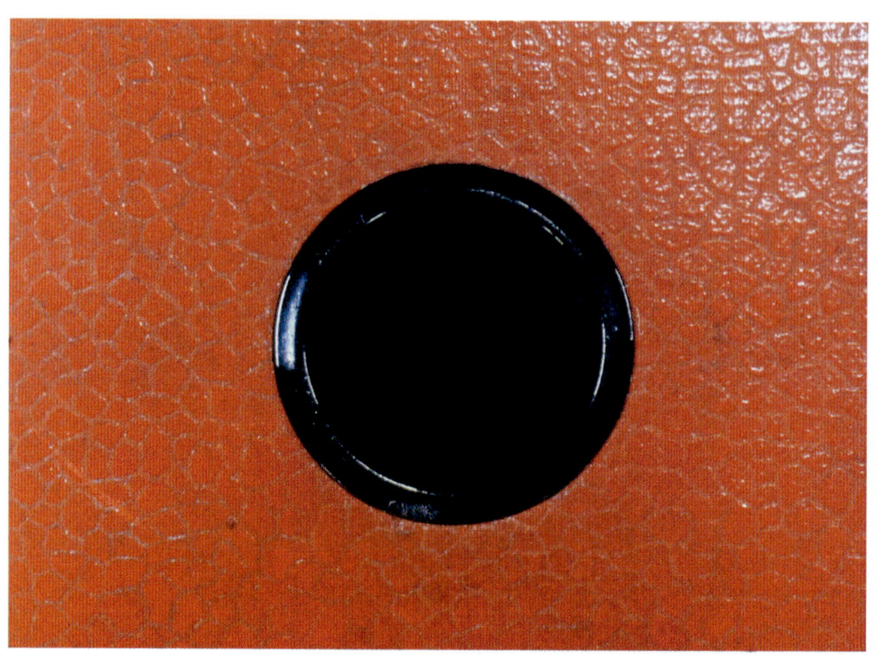

At the hour of tea

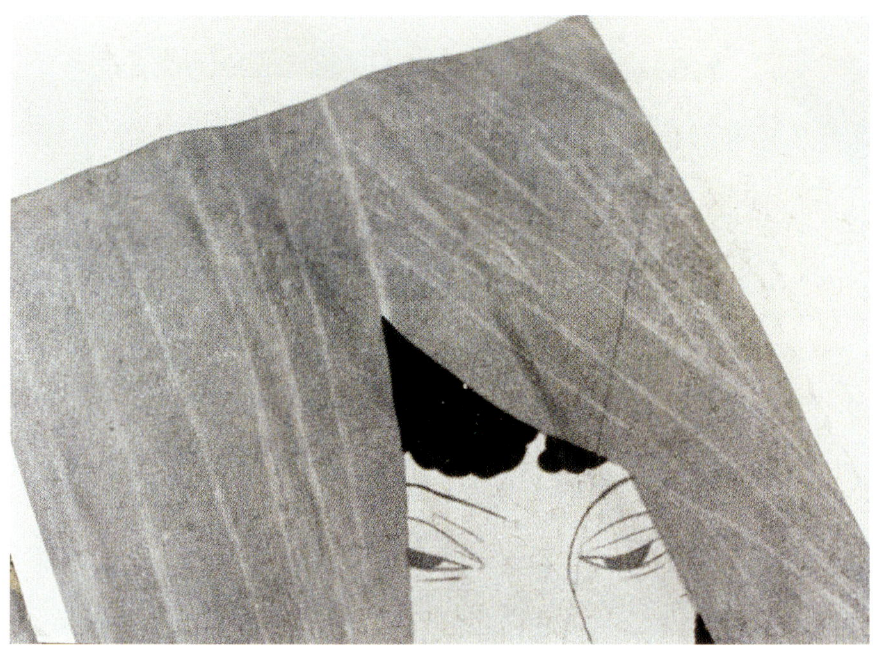

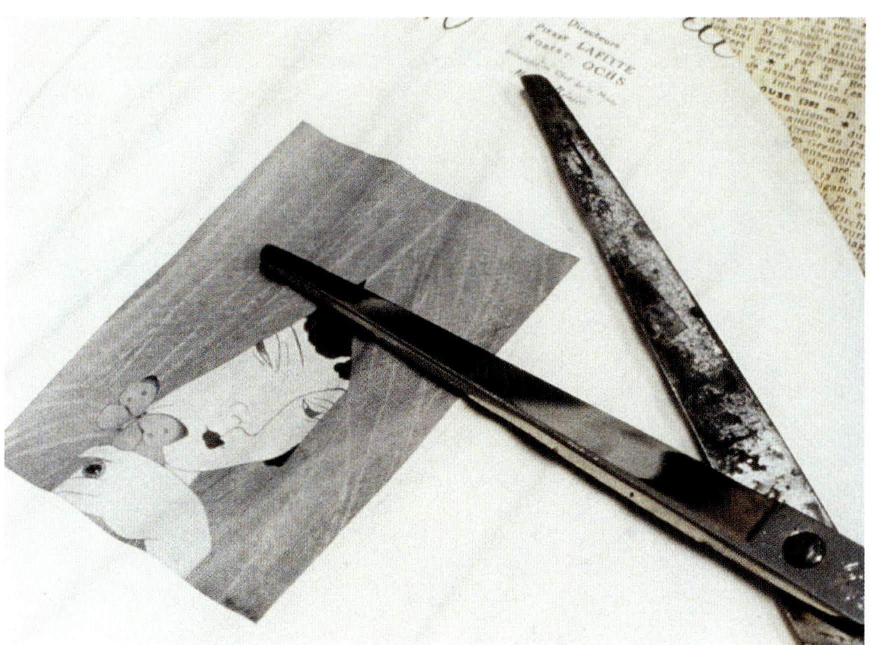

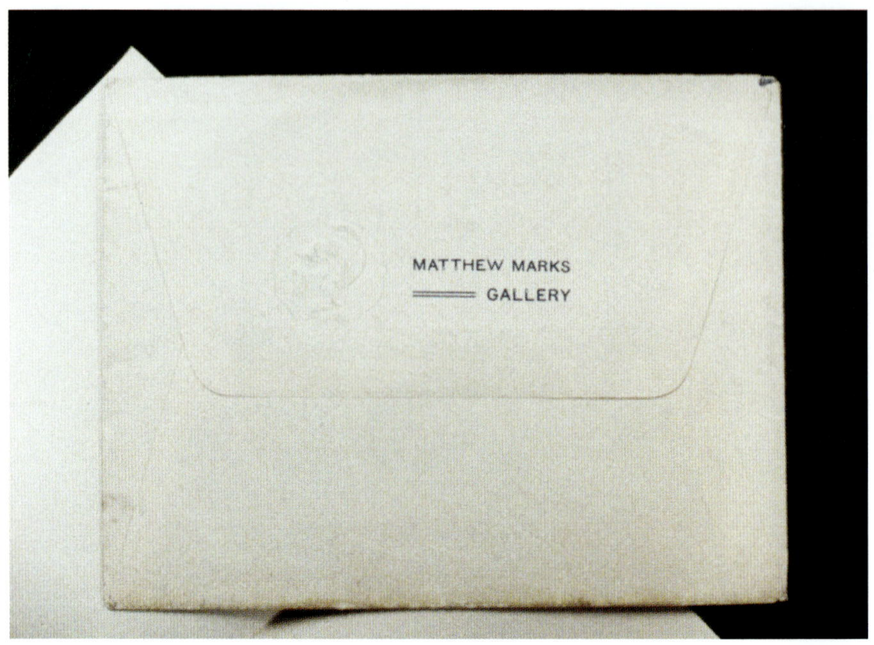

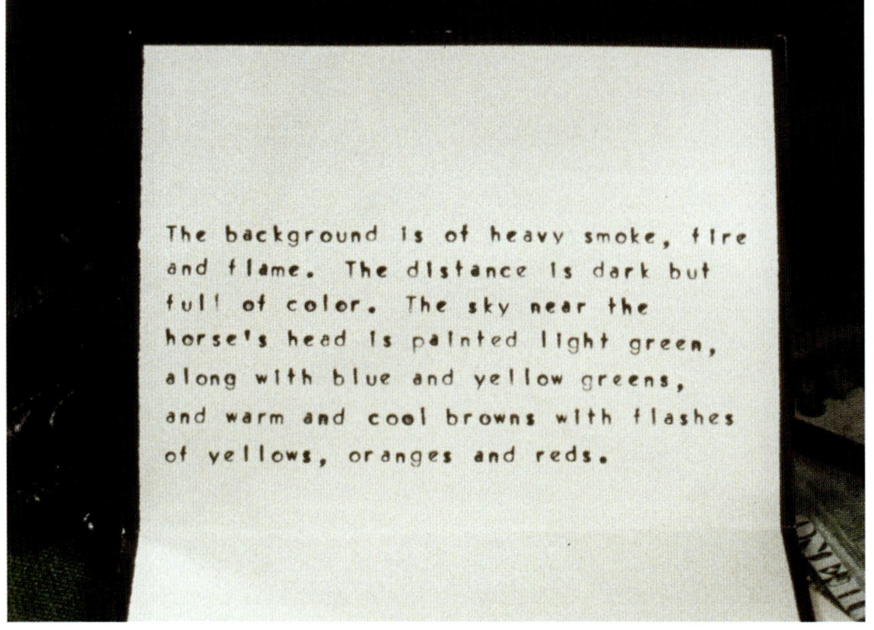

At the hour of tea

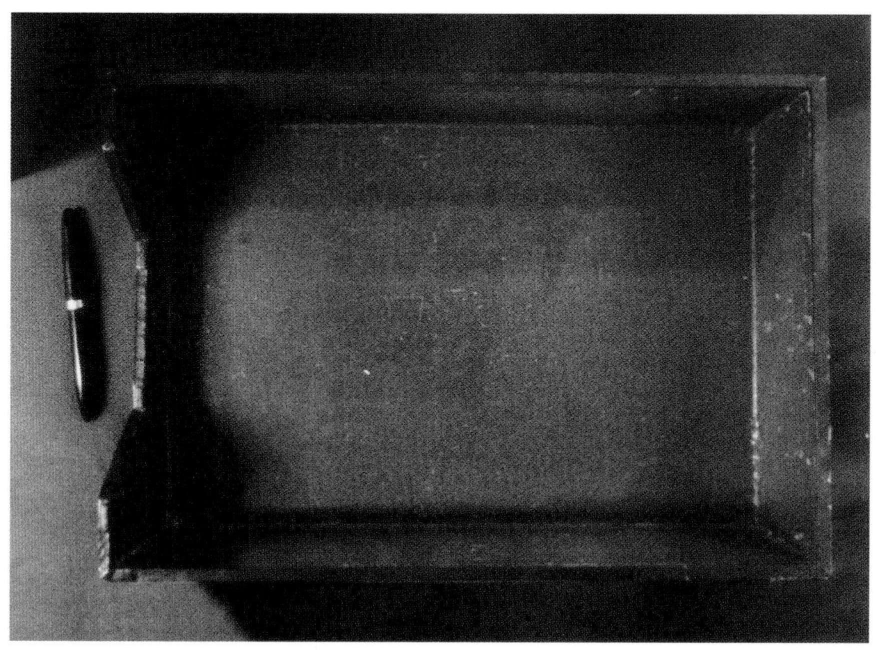

SEVEN FILMS BY PAUL SIETSEMA
NORA BURNETT ABRAMS

Nora Burnett Abrams is Associate Curator at the Museum of Contemporary Art Denver.

Empire, 2002

Sietsema's *Empire* centers on a historical space: the living room of the Modernist art critic Clement Greenberg as pictured in a 1964 issue of *Vogue* magazine. The artist built the space sculpturally, specifically with the intent of capturing it via a wide-angle lens, in order to match the view offered by the published image. He began working on the film in the late 1990s—a moment when Greenberg's theories on flatness, medium specificity, and truth to materials had fully succumbed to Conceptual and Process art. The iconic nature of this singular figure and his profound impact on the direction and reception of postwar, avant-garde art prompted Sietsema to make Greenberg himself (as well as his engineered self-presentation via this interior) the subject of an exploratory artwork. Sietsema anchored the film around the idea that Greenberg's personal living space acts as a kind of anthropological and philosophical site, working through the real and imagined archive of materials contained within, and implicated by, this historical node.

Sietsema constructed each object and space in *Empire*, drawing on scores of images and wide-ranging aesthetic research into the tropes of historical avant-gardes and perceptual theory. Developed in the years between 1998 and 2002, just as discussions of virtual reality and the difference between virtual space and real space were coming to the fore, *Empire* explores the difference between constructed media spaces and simple, daily, phenomenological experience. The film collapses the distance between the imagined and the actual, pointing toward the constructed nature of history itself and providing a perceptually determined experience of each space. Everything in the film was made by hand in order to democratize the individual elements experientially, and also to create a chain of production with many points at which to employ appropriated aesthetics productively. Sietsema has noted, "Abstraction and representation, true space and depicted space, [and] historical content from a range of time periods [are] all equalized through the making and filming to create another space not tied to the real world and not purely fantasy."[1]

Sietsema constructed the space of Greenberg's living room as a sculpture in his studio to be examined through repeated pans of his 16-millimeter Bolex, itself a defining tool of several generations of avant-garde movements. The camera makes geometric sweeps of the room, beginning with a close-up of a Barnett Newman "zip" painting, then slowly pulling back to encompass the entire space and its books, furniture, and art. The camera movement at one point traces the perimeter of a Donald Judd box sculpture, the size and shape of which closely resemble Sietsema's construction of the room in his studio. This section is filmed in such a way that the image matches the "color clear" hue of the color-negative camera original. The film is printed using reversal printing, which, as a positive-to-positive process, retains this color (which is normally lost in negative-to-positive printing). This infrastructural/technical color range plays on Greenberg's truth-to-materials modernist dictum, here applied structurally to the filmmaking process. In these ways, *Empire* employs film itself to address the imminent collapse of Greenberg's influence over advanced painting and sculpture. The title refers not only to Greenberg's critical reign but also to Andy Warhol's 1964 film of the same name, a key component of the Pop machinery that would soon initiate Greenberg's descent into obsolescence.

Empire contains a second historical space, again built by Sietsema specifically to be filmed: the Salon de la Princesse in the Hôtel de Soubise, an 18th-century Rococo salon that now houses France's national archives. The physical constructions made for *Empire* act as way stations to the final experiential filmic images, and the making of these objects in turn provided deep research that guided the way they are filmed. This Rococo salon is the aesthetic "sliding scale" alternative to the chronologically pinpointed quality of Greenberg's room. Greenberg's room has been defined by the specific instant of the *Vogue* photograph, whereas the Hôtel de Soubise is an example of the achronic in that the space, every detail of which has remained constant for almost 300 years, is itself nearly as static as a photograph. In the opening scenes of this section, the oval space of Sietsema's construction is filmed in a seemingly endless pan, showcasing the Salon's multitude of facing mirrors and subsequent reflections and regressions. Through this investigation of the Salon's *mise en abyme*, Sietsema links the space to its historical age, in which our conception of the infinite was first developed. The origins of the Enlightenment and the roots of modern philosophy, which would ultimately inform Greenberg's own polemics, are bound up in these Rococo aesthetics. Both the Salon's interior and Greenberg's Modernist space, separated as they are in time and space, signal high points in aesthetic history. This disparate pairing maps the larger shift of artistic interest from Paris to New York and from architecture to painting in the 1940s, 1950s, and 1960s.

Other sections of the film engage spatial theory and philosophies of virtual space without the allusion to architecture. They serve as multifaceted explorations of the formal tropes of Cubism and other aesthetic moments recognizable to the eyes and mind. Sietsema conceived of an organic-looking sculpture whose surface is pocked with deep crevices as a hybrid object: He brought a lost sculpture by Jackson Pollock (extant only in a photograph) together with a 1964 sculpture by Louise Bourgeois, shown in the same year and by the same gallery as Warhol's *Empire*, as well as the various study models Frederick Kiesler made for his *Endless House* project. The organic formalism of these sculptures and spaces has been implemented in association with utopian social ideals, ranging from primitivism in the 1920s and 1930s to *forme libre* of the 1940s, 1950s, and 1960s. Sietsema was intrigued by how this aesthetic could remain so consistent over such an extended period, and repeatedly deliver what was considered to be a primary, authentic, primitive spatial experience.

Yet another section of the film features a geometric structure made of thin black sticks. Line-to-line constructions such as this illustrate the most basic foundation for spatial modeling, a nod to the perceptual/phenomenological studies Sietsema researched as an extension of his investigation into historical avant-gardes. He develops this idea further in a segment that focuses on a crystalline structure, constructed from a cluster of transparent film gels. In filming this object, Sietsema exposed various shots over one another up to eight times, collapsing various stretches of time into a single experiential moment. This technique was first developed by Modernist photographers and filmmakers such as László Moholy-Nagy, Man Ray, and Jean Cocteau, who were exploring theories of the fourth dimension and collapsible time via the technical and mechanical processes of film. Sietsema's incorporation of these filming methods, enabled by the specific functions of the historical camera he was using, embed these two sculptures into the mechanics of the camera and the extended aesthetics of Greenberg's critical realm.

Empire begins with a completely dark frame that, as the camera's aperture opens, slowly reveals an image of a grasshopper. It is actually a black-and-white photograph of another sculpture constructed in Sietsema's studio. The filmic depiction of a still image inverts the usual function of film: to capture movement. In this segment, the opening of the camera's aperture to take in the image is the only action. The constructed insect rests on a branch, its leaf-like wings revealing the ways in which it has evolved to mimic its natural habitat and thus protect itself from predators. This natural mimesis points toward Sietsema's own inclination to replicate the forms he wishes to document on film. The grasshopper's adaptation to its environment also inverts the impact of the *Vogue* photograph of Greenberg's living room, as the critic's ideology, represented by this image, was circulated and thus became a point of aesthetic influence and mimicry for his discipline and for culture at large.

1. Conversation with the author, May 18, 2014.

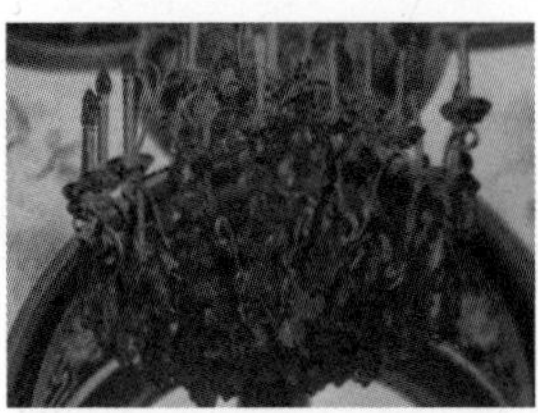

Empire, 2002
16mm film, no sound, 24 min.

PP. 25–40

Figure 3, 2008

Figure 3 presents and explores, in a format resembling both an art historical slide show and an ethnographic archive, a series of objects constructed by Sietsema in his studio. While making the film, Sietsema collected information about Pacific and Oceanic cultural artifacts of the 17th and 18th centuries, focusing on those retrieved on the first visits to the islands by Westerners. His intent was to investigate cultural production in an anti-iconic, pre-capitalist form. He looked at the early interminglings of these "innocent" objects and the value, rarity, and exoticism applied to them when inserted into the Western world, with its institutions and technologies (of which photography is primary). Photographic technology and distribution (via image-based sales catalogs) were essential in the recontextualization of these artifacts into Western culture and their initiation into art-objecthood. They would eventually find their way into private collections, leading to the formation of the modern museum.

The objects presented in the film include fishing nets, carrying straps, ceramic vessels, and bowls, among other items. The value of these tools in their native cultures depended solely upon their material utility, rather than abstract concepts of rarity or authorship. Their identification as art objects or collectible goods only emerged upon their introduction into Western civilization, with its capitalist system and attendant relationship between producer and consumer. By focusing on them, Sietsema complicates the dynamic of artistic value and authorship.

The objects in the film evolved in his studio, starting as source images and ending up as three-dimensional constructions. Sietsema accessed the utility of history by using printer's ink and plaster, among other materials, to bring his constructions to life while, paradoxically, having them match the perimeter of the original objects. As part of the process, he incorporated key materials used in anthropological recording and photography, for instance plaster, aluminum powder, and gum arabic. These materials are traditionally used to make imprints of non-transportable surfaces, to make light reflect better on dark surfaces so that an object will be more photographable, and to temporarily reassemble broken objects in the field without doing further damage. Rather than creating illusion through representation alone, Sietsema also conceived of his object making as a form of concrete depiction, one in which the production chain of the image is rife with conceptually or culturally loaded techniques and methods. In one example, he crafted an object resembling a New Guinea carrying strap out of tape and newspaper. After covering the object in thick, flame-retardant white paint, he used a blowtorch to burn the interior newspaper away, leaving only a bright white shell, making a nearly self-luminous physical imprint of the object before its eventual two-dimensional imprinting into the emulsion of the film stock.

The artist's additional use of Hydrocal (a type of white gypsum cement) and other materials in *Figure 3* derived not only from his investigation of anthropological photography and recording, but also rather synergistically from Postminimalism and artists such as Richard Serra, Eva Hesse, and Robert Morris, who worked with plainspoken industrial materials and acted upon them in much the same way that the islanders used their own local materials. Postminimal artists often allowed their materials to determine their eventual forms and frequently manipulated them with their hands at a time when computer-assisted manufacturing was becoming the dominant mode of industrial production. Similarly, the islanders used available materials and manipulated them by hand. These objects' designs also derived largely from the materials themselves, without the influence of proprietary design or built-in obsolescence that capitalism prescribes.

By combining these various methods, *Figure 3* reflects Sietsema's interest in producing an artwork that represents the pre-historical and post-historical eras, and bypasses the recent historical phase. The current mass availability of historical aesthetics and images has created an echo chamber that blurs and displaces the link between an image and its chronology, origin, and materiality. The film presents objects that embody both the island cultures' direct relationship with their material objects and the unregulated proliferation of information and images that have allowed distinctions of chronology and geography to become ever more fluid.

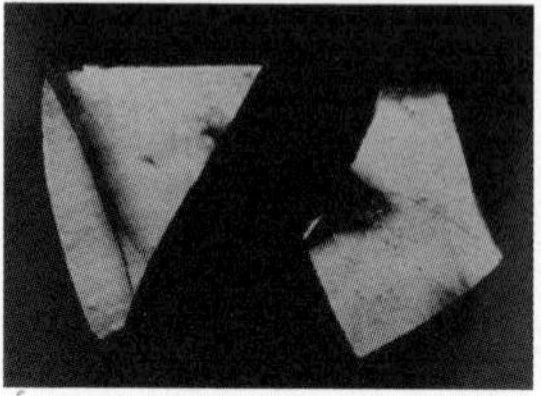

Figure 3, 2008
16mm film, no sound, 16 min.

PP. 43–56

Anticultural Positions, 2009

Sietsema's 2009 film *Anticultural Positions* was presented as a lecture by the artist at The New School in New York on February 23, 2009, at 6:30 p.m. while the artist himself was on a plane back to the West Coast. For Sietsema, the standard "artist's lecture" is a questionable cultural convention in which the speech of the artist is meant to do work that artworks themselves should be doing. As a result, the talk can create a kind of redundancy that undermines the integrity of the work. Thus, rather than delivering a standard slide presentation on his work, Sietsema created a film based on the structure of an artist's lecture. The film intersperses what appear to be abstract painted images with entirely black frames in which a text runs along the bottom, like subtitles.

Sietsema, who had begun "collecting" artists' lectures prior to this film, based the text on a lecture given at the Arts Club of Chicago by Jean Dubuffet in December 1951. Sietsema altered the text to describe his own practice more accurately but left the language of this other era as it was. Dubuffet's text outlined his complete rejection of the Western canon and its outmoded ideas of beauty. Partly confessional and partly instructive, it attacked artistic conventions and strictures while championing formlessness and ambiguity as vital components of the artistic process.

The imagery depicted in *Anticultural Positions* resembles the style and materiality of Dubuffet's own *art brut* painting, but in actuality it shows details of various work surfaces from Sietsema's studio. As research for the project, Sietsema studied many publications on postwar abstract painting, including *Quadrum* magazine, which was produced from 1956 to 1966. The presentation of abstract art in its pages deeply informed how Sietsema framed and recorded the images of his work surfaces in *Anticultural Positions*. The marks, accretions, and traces visible in the film are the physical remains of Sietsema's film works created during the previous decade, and his visual presentation of them within the film operates as a material replacement for discussing the work. In this sense, and as the standard form of a lecture would ascribe, *Anticultural Positions* encompasses all of the artist's major works made through 2009.

Anticultural Positions captures the earnestness and polemical vehemence of Dubuffet's treatise—qualities themselves which, attached to two-dimensional formal investigations, are relics of the era. Although the text could be seen as explicating the images shown throughout the film, it functions more as a cultural artifact than as a directive or a proposition for Sietsema or his work. The artist reanimates and retools the text into a material in dialogue with his own practice, as well as an exploration of the relationship between historical material and contemporary modes of media.

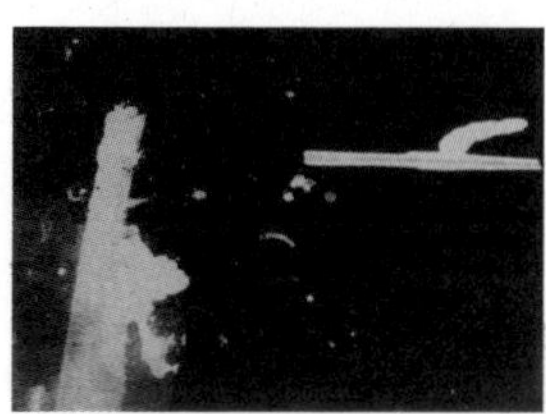

Anticultural Positions, 2009
16mm film, no sound, 30 min.

PP. 59–70

Encre chine, 2012

Encre chine presents a range of studio-related objects covered in a black, slightly reflective substance. This substance is *encre de Chine*, a black etching ink that is thick and viscous. Hovering between liquid and solid, the ink acts as a democratizing agent in the film, encasing the objects and the surfaces on which they rest so thoroughly that the items can be identified only by their contours. The film moves between detailed close-ups of specific objects—various tools, parts of a disassembled picture frame, a canister of 35-millimeter film—and broader shots of a studio-like mise-en-scène. The artist deaccessioned these items from his studio and, utilizing this heavy coating of ink, effectively transformed them from objects to images by suppressing their original materiality and function.

The artist used *encre de Chine* in part to form a linkage to the filmic medium itself. As he has noted, "I like to think of the

129

emulsion coating 16-millimeter film, a viscous liquid that has become fixed. This chemical/material coating reacts physically to light in specific ways, developing an image. The ink coating the objects both obscures them and also forces an attention on the part of the viewer that helps to capture characteristics that would otherwise escape a conscious read. The light-absorbing thick ink has a parallel in the 16-millimeter prints of this film, which are very dense with emulsion, blocking much more light than usual from passing through the physical filmstrip. The film begins to become opaque, which is a quality *Encre chine* has as well."[1] With the thicker emulsion, Sietsema introduces a material linkage between the processes of 16-millimeter film and the objects of a studio, between earthly functional objects and the world of images and image production.

At the time he made *Encre chine*, Sietsema was investigating John Searle's "Chinese Room" thought experiment. This experiment studied the distinctions between a computer's ability to translate between languages and its inability to truly "understand" them or be capable of consciousness. Sietsema was interested in how this experiment might be transferred to the camera, which "translates" images in a similar way. *Encre chine* serves in part as Sietsema's investigation into the chemical and mechanical processes of the camera and the linkages between those and the objects captured on film, ultimately exploring the possibility of a machine language as such.

1. Adam Szymczyk and Quinn Latimer, "Impossibly Clean Models: Paul Sietsema in Conversation" in *Paul Sietsema: Interviews on Films and Works*, ed. Quinn Latimer (Berlin: Sternberg Press, 2012), 105.

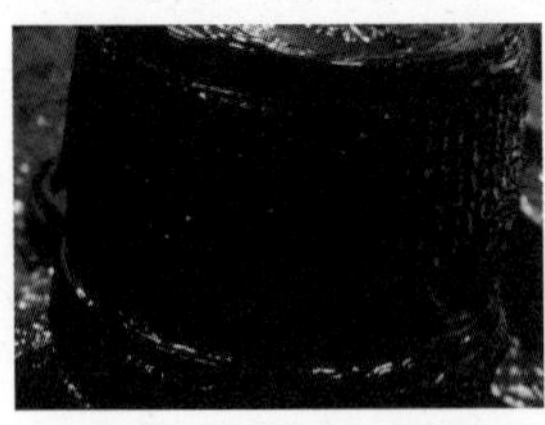

Encre chine, 2012
16mm film, no sound, 15 min.

PP. 73–80

Telegraph, 2012

Telegraph explores the idea of an artwork as a transmission—a conduit through which messages can be sent across time—by utilizing basic materials to embody language. In the film, Sietsema uses found shards of wood to form an alphabet. Connected through a series of dissolves, the scraps of wood are configured and reconfigured piece by piece in a sequence that slowly spells out the phrase "L/E/T/T/E/ R/T/O/A/Y/O/U/N/G/P/A/I/N/T/E/R." The materiality of the wood invites an experience of surface and color that diminishes linguistic legibility and its associative order, emphasizing instead the inherent abstraction of each letterform.

The wood was gathered by the artist over time, from disparate places and sources. There are pieces of a trellis from a previous studio, parts of houses in which he has lived, wood he found between his car and his studio, and wood his friend found littering the landscape in New Orleans after Hurricane Katrina. These shards migrated from trees to become planks, then buildings, before ultimately returning to a state of pure material again, an encultured journey alluded to and replayed by their formation into letters in *Telegraph*.

Presented in both typical and atypical orientations, each letter is an abstract image as much as a shape to be read or decoded, and each configuration functions more as a visual marker than as a carrier of meaning. In its movement toward language, each piece of wood changes radically from its origin while also remaining constant, its objecthood ineradicable. As the artist has noted, it is "something that comes close to but perhaps does not quite take form enough to qualify as 'something' in a cultural sense, as a language, [or as] anything else."[1]

The artist appropriated the missive "L/E/T/T/E/R/T/O/A/Y/O/ U/N/G/P/A/I/N/T/E/R" from the collected correspondence between the writer Rainer Maria Rilke and the aspiring poet Franz Kappros. Sietsema conceived of the phrase as a directive to a formalist painter whose minimal work resembles the formations of wood shards in the film and who died at a young age during the 1970s. By addressing this relationship, which is both real and imaginary, Sietsema shifts the content of the phrase from an elder to a younger artist and instead conceives of an interchange existing outside of chronological time—much like an image, or the aesthetic flow between generations in art making. The film thus stands in the center of an ever-shifting matrix, with both Sietsema and the painter slipping between the roles of older and younger artist, and receiver and sender. Sietsema is punning on the word "medium," as he uses the film itself as a way to communicate with the dead, again harnessing the artwork's ability to embody disparate historical moments simultaneously.

Sietsema once said of this film, "The piece has no real subject matter: it's just a kind of transmission. The concrete history of its objects are related by the random character of contingency rather than by a formalized intention."[2] *Telegraph* transmits a message,

131

but, ultimately, the crafting of the message and the way in which the viewer must actively assemble it are the real subjects of the film.

1. Conversation with the author, May 31, 2014.
2. Adam Szymczyk and Quinn Latimer, "Impossibly Clean Models: Paul Sietsema in Conversation" in *Paul Sietsema: Interviews on Films and Works*, ed. Quinn Latimer (Berlin: Sternberg Press, 2012), 96.

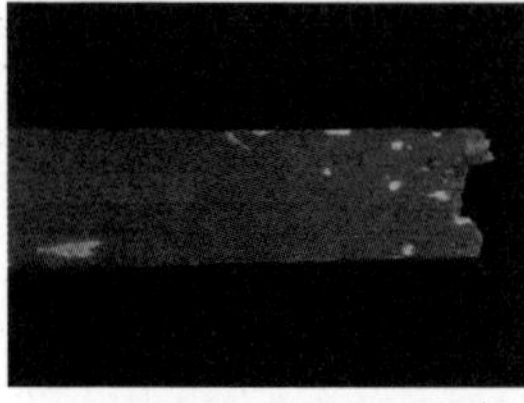

Telegraph, 2012
16mm film, no sound, 12 min.

PP. 83–90

The sentence, 2012

The sentence presents a succession of close-ups of a rough-hewn, granite-like surface on which words appear one or two at a time. Granite traditionally functions as a sculptural material into which facts or memorials are carved or etched, as on a cornerstone or a tombstone. In this film, however, Sietsema uses the surface as a blank page to be inscribed with a seemingly handwritten text, thus conflating forms of public and private discourse. Although the text appears to be instructive in nature, it ultimately proves to be a satirically invalid account of contemporary art practice.

The full text of *The sentence* reads:

> The/Sound/of/your/hammer/at/Five/in/the/Morning/or/Nine/
> at/Night/heard/by/a Critic/makes/him/easy/Six/Months/
> longer/But/if he/sees/you/at/a/Billiard/Table or/hears/your/
> Voice/in/a/Tavern/when/you/should/be/at/Work/he/sends/
> for/his Quill/and/Well/the/next/Day

It is an alteration of a quote by Benjamin Franklin about the relationship between a creditor and a debtor: Indications of labor or production offer relief to the creditor, but any sign of leisure or irreverence creates anxiety, leading to an immediate demand for payment. The film's title alludes both to the threat of debtor's prison that was common in Franklin's time as well as to the form the adage takes: a single sentence.

For this film, Sietsema adjusts the relationship between the two parties from that of debtor and creditor to that of artist and critic. The artist at work assuages fear and mitigates risk, but the artist at leisure causes that risk to spike. *The sentence* addresses, in stark terms, the effect of market forces on the ways in which art is produced and consumed today. In translating the adage to the context of a post-Fordist, capitalist art market, however, the rule collapses. The notion that increased labor or productivity would assuage any concern on the part of a critic is defunct in today's art world. Sietsema suggests that the direct link between the type of physical productivity alluded to in the adage and artistic value is no longer extant and that, in an inversion of Franklin's original formula, social labor is now privileged above physical labor.

By translating the sentence from a written text to a time-based series of projected images, Sietsema reorients the meaning of this passage in terms that engage with the economics of the contemporary art market, and its particular contingencies and debts. Entrenching Franklin's adage more fully in "material," the film points toward the decline in importance of material and form, as well as the manipulation of the two in today's art world. In parallel, the film investigates the contemporary economy of viewership. *The Sentence* recontextualizes Franklin's quote as a temporal phenomenon in which each constituent piece must be comprehended in turn, all while maintaining a view of the whole. A few moments of inattention on the part of a viewer, and the message is lost. In this way, the film stresses a type of active viewing, as the adage can only be apprehended as a whole through rather labor-intensive attentiveness. The film challenges the idea that the act of viewing is an act of leisure. It reanimates imperative viewing as a form of social conscience while shifting away from the inattentive consumption inherent in art that is associated with passive entertainment and capital gain.

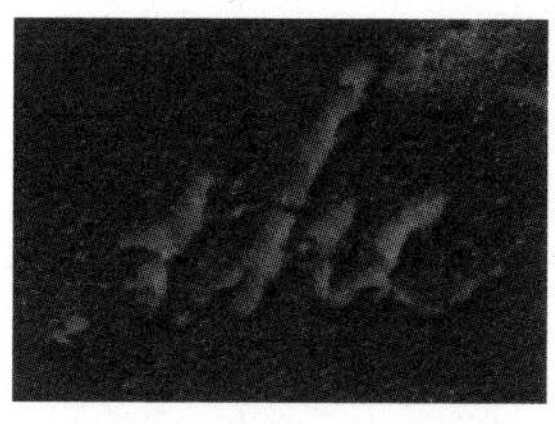

The sentence, 2012
16mm film, no sound, 10 min.

PP. 93–100

At the hour of tea, 2013

At the hour of tea presents a sequence of arranged objects of the type commonly seen on a desktop. With this film Sietsema brings the tools of the study or office together with objects of contemplation often found there, overlaying time periods within the perceptual matrix of a workstation. He was interested in formulating a translation made of objects from different eras, the images of which have made their way into the virtual desktop as common symbols for the activities they represent.

He employs a language of clichéd "collectible" objects—Roman glass, coins, minor antiquities, and the like—both to invoke the idea of a salon or space of contemplation as a parallel to the contemporary studio, and to suggest a kind of leisure-based consumptive creativity more commonly shared by present-day producers and consumers of culture. The film uses these objects to reference the work or production that takes place in the studio. Sietsema has noted that he was interested in "the idea of things that are done outside of work being made in a work, becoming a mechanism for collecting and displaying different aspects of daily work life."[1] The clock, the calendar, and the dates on the magazines register this most explicitly, as they collectively track the time involved in the making of the film, which, after these collected productive moments, becomes locked into the eternal replay that is the nature of the medium.

At certain moments during the film, a text emerges on a white card with a black printed border. Such stationery has historically been used to announce a death; in the film, however, it presents the reader with a formalist, Modernist description of a 19th-century painting. Appropriated from a college paper written by the artist Ad Reinhardt in the 1940s, it brings a painting from the past to life, inverting the historical function of such an announcement.

Another inversion performed in the film is the use of past historical objects to define the present. Sietsema uses the arrangement of collected objects to produce the projected creative field as a mirror of his own work life. Drawing on the idea of skeuomorphism common in modern computer interfaces, Sietsema fills his tableaux with now-outmoded items that live on as mere icons of their former functions: for instance an envelope that now denotes email, or the continued use of the word "inbox" despite the obsolescence of the actual object. At the same time, other objects function as historical analogues to their counterparts in a modern workspace, including the typewriter (succeeded by the computer) and a vintage film camera (now replaced by the proliferation of digital images). The combination of these items in the tableaux creates a blurring—between past and present, and among the objects, their symbols, and their functions.

A green felt-like material is the background against which Sietsema films many of his objects. The baize, which is also used on billiard and card tables, is another marker of the distinction between leisure and labor. Sietsema has noted that, historically, this material was used to cover the doors separating masters and servants. It marks differences in class, a point reinforced by its proximity to other luxury items that reiterate this evocation of class difference in the film. The film's title, lifted from a newspaper clipping that appears in one of the sequences, also references class. "At the hour of tea" alludes to a nonspecific time: general within a single day, but also general across the many years of this social tradition. In so doing, the title defines the time of the film, Sietsema notes, "culturally rather than numerically."[2] Each segment of the film closes with an image of an actual green leatherette inbox. The tableau, having been examined by the camera, is now depicted as a physical printed photograph, an object itself, which is deposited into the inbox—the image constructed, consumed, and dispatched.

1. Conversation with the author, May 18, 2014.
2. Paul Sietsema and Lynn Warren, "Interview with Paul Sietsema," in the special publication accompanying *Paul Sietsema* (Chicago: MCA Chicago, 2013), 8.

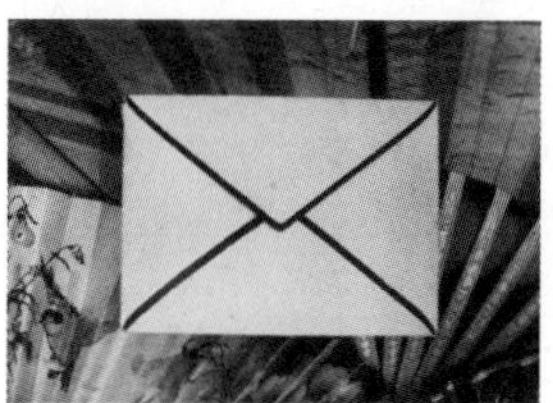

At the hour of tea, 2013
16mm film, no sound, 17 min.

PP. 103–119

Seven Films by Paul Sietsema

Published on the occasion of the exhibition
Paul Sietsema: Films and Works
Museum of Contemporary Art Denver
July 2–October 12, 2014

Co-published by MCA Denver and Mousse Publishing, Milan
www.mcadenver.org
www.moussepublishing.com

Generous funding for this publication was provided by Baryn Futa
and Matthew Marks Gallery, New York / Los Angeles.

The Museum of Contemporary Art Denver would also like to thank the citizens of the
Scientific and Cultural Facilities District for their support.

Editorial coordination: Stefano Cernuschi
Copy editor: Lindsey Westbrook
Proofreading: Amanda Glesmann
Design: Studio Mousse - Marco Fasolini, Fausto Giliberti, Matteo Gualandris,
Massimiliano Pace, Francesco Valtolina

First edition of 1000

Printed in Italy

Paul Sietsema would like to thank: Nora Burnett Abrams, Aurime Aleksandraviciute,
George Baker, Jack Bankowsky, Christopher Bedford, Andrew Berardini, Ariana Beyn,
Manuel Borja-Villel, Helen Brown, Cornelia Butler, Stefano Cernuschi, Suzanne
Cotter, Michelle Cotton, David Crane, Eric Crosby, Donna De Salvo, Ann Demeester,
Deutscher Akademischer Austausch Dienst (DAAD), Apsara DiQuinzio, Mary
Doyle, Anne Ellegood, Eva Fabbris, Elena Filipovic, Douglas Fogle, Foundation for
Contemporary Arts, John Simon Guggenheim Memorial Foundation, Gary Garrels,
Sherri Geldin, Yoann Gourmel, Tim Griffin, Madeleine Grynsztejn, Bruce Hainley,
Jan Hoet, Michael Ned Holte, Suzanne Hudson, Chrissie Iles, Giovanni Intra, Adam
Lerner, Kate Macfarlane, Matthew Marks, Philippe Alain Michaud, Alexander Overduin,
Cornelis Overduin, Lisa Overduin, Brent Petersen, Ann Philbin, Nina Pohl, Lawrence
Rinder, Adrian Rosenfeld, Elodie Royer, Paul Schimmel, Fabian Schöneich, Sandra
Shelley, Sarah Robayo Sheridan, Ellsworth Overduin Sietsema, Erik Sietsema, Jay &
Asa Sietsema, Lukas Sietsema, Debra Singer, Katharine Stout, Ali Subotnick, Adam
Szymczyk, Dean Valentine, Lynne Warren, Suzanne Weaver, Wexner Center Residency
Artist Award, Robin Wright, and Jonas Zakaitis.

ISBN: 978-88-6749-100-1   € 26 – $ 35